To: Sharul

MW01268314

WHEN YOU THINK NO ONE IS WATCHING

Wild But True Hotel Stories

EMMANUEL GRATZIMI

PARENTAL GUIDANCE ADVISED

Emmanuel
Gratzimi

Printed in the United States of America

ISBN-13: 978-1540423856

PUBLISHING

LET THE WORDS CHANGE YOU

Made in the USA
Charleston, SC
12 December 2016

Sources

(I)@Justia.com, *Criminal Law-Robbery*, www.Justia.com , Published 2016 https://www.justia.com/criminal/docs/uniform-crime-reporting-handbook/robbery.html Accessed 09 November 2016.

(II)Smith, Adam. *Wealth of Nations*, edited by C. J. Bullock. Vol. X. The Harvard Classics. New York: P.F. Collier & Son, 1909–14; Bartleby.com, 2001.

enhance your intellectual and decision making processes. Every story we create for others by our actions has the possibility to provide a negative or positive example of behavior.

Concluding Thoughts

I want to end by thanking you the reader for allowing me the opportunity, through *When You Think No One Is Watching*, to provide for your entertainment a gambit of emotional odysseys.

When You Think No One Is Watching has offered an exploration into the untold true stories which occur daily in the hotel industry. The intervals which hotel employees share with their visitors are momentary, however, it allows for a unique opportunity to glimpse into the lives of the guests served. As a result, those employed experience the joys, sorrows, terrors, and elations of the guests they interact with. Each work day provides a differing story which can range from absurd hilarity to the very darkest of tales.

Although evil and tragedy occur commonly, and cannot always be completely deterred, it is the upmost desire of most luxury hotel employees that your wellbeing and safe amusement be of paramount importance. Wickedness can occur in any location, and the more troubling stories described in *When You Think No One Is Watching*, should not defer your ambitions of exploration. Most rational persons desire admiration more than indulging in undesirable personal fantasies.

It is my sincerest desire that the small portions of wisdom, founded by personal experience, which were offered in during the course of the book, stimulate and

Table of Contents

Introduction

In my near decade of experience employed in law enforcement at upscale convention hotels as well as luxury resorts, I have had the unique opportunity to witness and to interact with a full spectrum of individuals. These individuals range from billionaires to politicians to drug addicts, criminals and the bazaar individuals who fit somewhere in between. I have witnessed people at their highest and their lowest moments.

These Wild but True Stories include moments which will cause you to laugh, cringe and cry. This book covers stories which go from humorous to dark. Hotel guests are but a microcosm of the people we meet every day. They are the people who we go to school, party, lunch and work with but also people who we really don't know because we can't see what they do when they think no one is watching.

It is important to note that only the events and not the names of the persons are shared because of privacy. Also, most of these stories are for an adult audience. Parental guidance is recommended.

CHAPTER 1

Who's Fooling Who?

The Drunk Senator

One of the many benefits to working at an upscale hotel is the ability to personally meet and interact with celebrities. While the media can project either a positive or negative image of an individual, interacting with a person you supposed you already knew is an amusing experience of its own accord.

On this particular wintery weekend, the hotel was bursting with dignitaries, corporate business men, lobbyists, and politicians. A major political group scheduled an event and reserved the entire hotel and convention hall. Most were coming from different parts of the world with their commercial and political agendas in tow. Meetings, as well as networking events, were scheduled to occur in various parts of the hotel. The sponsored events were varied to enable attendees to have time to establish political, business, and personal relationships.

Coming in that day, most of the hotel security staff assumed we would be coordinating heavily with the Secret Service and private security members to maintain the privacy of the attendees. Some of the meetings were convened as invite only and the attendees were carefully selected and screened. Security was established so that those wishing to access some areas of the hotel needed to show proper identification.

In the midst of the seriousness of those that we were protecting that day, I was dispatched to go to the water fountain at the hotel's entrance to handle an elderly man who was stripping off his clothes and walking in the water. As I arrived on the scene, I found myself having to move through several of his comrades. They were slurring "twenty one" in a drunken unified chorus.

As I approached the man, he was knee deep in the fountain's water and was using one of his hands to struggle with the last button of his white, fitted, black tie, dress shirt. With his other hand, he was attempting to hold on to the fountains sculpture for support. His wet and wrinkled fingers were barely grasping the button as he tried to push it forward through the shirt's buttonhole.

As I stepped close to the fountain to speak to him, he momentarily paused and giggled. Leaning forward from the water, he stumbled to remain balanced as he whispered to my nose. Entirely oblivious to the fact that he was not speaking into my ear, he told me not to worry because he was the second coming of Jesus and was going to walk nude on water. From the way he smelled, I really wasn't entirely sure whether he had indeed been drinking or if the powers that be had replaced the fountain's water with pure unfiltered clear moonshine. Either way, at this point I was ecstatic. It had all the makings of a fun afternoon.

One of the hotel bartenders, came out with the man's bar bill in hand and informed me that the man owed the hotel bar for the 21 shots of whisky he consumed. As the man hadn't died immediately, it seemed apparent to me that this old man's liver and brain must in fact be a hardened veteran of years of alcohol abuse. This theory would soon be disproven.

His friends stared drunkenly at however many images they saw of me with distain as I talked the man out of the fountain, and quickly escorted him out of the cold, through a back corridor, and into the main security office. This was not only to monitor his well-being, and to provide medical assistance, I was also attempting to not to disturb the other more somber politicians and corporate persons present.

The man's reasoning ability was now completely gone. Once in the office, I provided him with all the comforts a drunken man could desire. I and coworker sat the man down on a chair neighboring a desk and provided him with a trash can. This provided him something to lean on and to house his vomit.

He cried out hysterically when I asked for his name or identification badge. He couldn't remember his own name. I had to explain to him that without identification, we couldn't identify anyone that might be able to assist him. He found this notion extremely disturbing, and he attempted to force his brain recollection as he stared into the trash can we had provided for him.

Leaning over lousily, his wallet slipped from his pants onto the floor. This was a proverbial jackpot for me. As I picked through it in an attempt to identify the man, I found a business card with a man's face on it. "That's my assistant, and he's not banging his wife," the man screamed at me as I held the card up for him to identify. I held my palms over my mouth to contain the growing ear to ear to grin on my face. Using the business card, the man's assistant was called and asked to come to the main security office.

I then happened to find a hidden government ID with the aged man's picture on it. "That's it, my name", the man yelled. "I'm a Senator up for re-election." With this, my amusement was almost at a tipping point; however, I contained myself with short puffs of laughter. My apparent pleasure upset the senator and he took my amusement as a disbelief in his abilities. Indignantly, he attempted to regain an appearance of an upstanding statesman, "Vote for me," he pathetically begged looking up at my chin from his seat.

Hearing me let loose another one of my short puffs, the man stood to deliver a speech as to why he needed both my and my coworker's vote for the upcoming election and why he was the best candidate. Mid speech, a steady stream of vomit projected from his mouth momentarily pausing his persuasive appeals. Puke landed directly on one of my female coworkers as she rushed in to assist him. She had previously told me she wanted to look "extra special" for the politicians.

Instead, she becomes an unintended receptacle for the Senator's bile and she left squealing out of the room as her makeup, clothes and hair are coated in a layer of vomit.

When the Senators' assistant comes through the door, I am bent over, grabbing my stomach belly laughing. Meanwhile, the senator wet and half naked, stumbles down into his own spew. This is now a full blown public relations nightmare of epic proportions that the assistant and hotel must manage. The assistant decides to demand emergency services. Upon their arrival, the Senator tries once again assume an appearance of dignity but is put on a stretcher with a thin medical blanket to cover his face and hurried through the back corridor into the ambulance. Onlookers were assured the Senator would be fine but was having some medical concerns.

I Do, I Will

The technological era that we are currently immersed in has provided humanity with many securities and advantages. We have become assured of our personal and financial protection through several digital monitoring systems. With mobile banking apps informing us instantly of purchases, transfers, and banking credits, we can now immediately identify and rectify amiss transactions.

Our survival of the fittest now rests in our ability to process data. Unfortunately for them, not everyone catches the same drift on the same wave. People's inability to adapt to the technological era has provided each of us with humorous stories. The proper use of technology sometime, however, can literally catch people, unbeknownst of its advantage, pants down.

It is mid-morning on a Monday and staff members in all of the various departments of the hotel have commenced normal day operations. I am in the security office joking around with my coworkers when I hear our office door slam. Looking over my shoulder, I see a housekeeper angrily storm into our main security office. She was almost fuming at the mouth; steam was nearly billowing from her eyes. She was followed quickly by an extremely young and nervous hotel café cashier. Beads of sweat clouded the young man's stringy hair.

In one hand, the housekeeper held a hotel café receipt, in the other, her smart phone. On her phone was a message from her bank notifying her of a nearly four hundred dollar debit on her account charged to her by the hotel. The transaction occurred almost immediately after she had gotten her morning specialty coffee. She returned to the hotel café, and furiously demanded that the young teen follow her into our office.

The housekeeper told us she was trying her best not to lose her job by creating a commotion, but demanded to know what type of con game the youngster was trying to run on her, and how he was expecting to reimburse her for the funds she presumed he had taken from her. The cashier, a teenager, still in high school and only working over the summer, was timidly trying to his best to explain that he had only charged her card what was on her receipt. He, teary eyed, explained that he would never try and charge anything more than the usual price, and he had no idea how or why she had the larger amount deducted from her bank.

Expecting for the confrontation to turn physical, the housekeeper began to remove her jewelry and place them behind our security counter in our lost and found tray. As each piece of jewelry clinked onto our metal tray, she sprouted out a new threat. The young man, after taking a brief minute to contemplate the scenario and his options, scurried across the room as we hurriedly got between him and the angry housekeeper.

We called for his department director and the front desk manager to assist us in reviewing the charges. After a brief internal investigation, it was discovered the housekeeper's name was reserved on a luxury suite in the hotel. Her debit card, which happened to be a joint account with her husband, had been used, and a key for the room had already been issued just a few minutes prior to her arrival at our office. In addition, it was discovered that the room had been reserved using the housekeeper's employee discount. She stated her daughter had access to all that information as her daughter had used the debit card and the employee discount on her vacation a month prior.

As it was her name on the room, the housekeeper furiously commanded the front office director have a key be made and issued to her. In so much that was indeed her name on the room and her employee discount had been used, the management staff decided they would not refuse to deny her access to the room. Henceforth, she was provided a key to the luxurious room.

We in the security staff followed behind her, sure we were about to prevent an ass whipping of an apocalyptic proportion. The housekeeper informed us that her daughter had probably returned with her college boyfriend.She told us that she distrusted her daughter's athlete boyfriend because one day, he probably would leave her daughter broken hearted. She would be damned if her daughter would be staying with him, using her hard earned money and her employee discount at her

job. She didn't care that her daughter was making a surprise early return.

Wwwwhhaaammmmm, the housekeeper barged through the guest room's door. The door hit the wall and launched itself back at us, hitting the housekeeper squarely in her stomach and chest making her awkwardly stumble into a fall in front of us. She slapped away a helping hand as one of our staff members bent to help her get up. We heard an "Oh my word" from a females voice, and surprised movements inside of the room. The woman's initial assumptions appeared to have been confirmed as we could both male and female voices.

Not wanting to break the door, the wall, or myself, I asked the lady, as she struggled to get back on her feet to regain her intimidating posture to step back so I could make a less resounding first entry. I used my master key to open the room. I immediately regretted my decision to enter the room in front of the housekeeper. If there is anything worse than a morally upright, happily married, mother walking in on her daughter having sex, it is that same woman walking in on her husband.

As we entered the room, there was a nearly empty wine bottle leaning off a dining cart filled with assorted caviar. This was, as we later found out, charged to the room. The dainties were followed by a trail of rose pedals leading to the woman's startled husband who was standing nude next to his naked lover. She was hiding herself underneath the bed's covers.

Caught, all her husband could think to do was to look innocently into his wife's shell shocked glare and say, "Oh hey honey, this is my coworker". To our surprise, his lover rolled out of the bed, wiggled her fingers at the wife, like a schoolgirl excited to see her best friend and began making her way across the room, arms and chest wide open to greet the wife. There are those among us who smile in the face of destruction.

For all the commotion that the wife had caused earlier, both in the office and on the elevator ride, her next move actually terrified me; there was no yelling, crying or even a demand for an explanation. The housekeeper, raised the phone, still in her hand, snapped a quick photo. She snickered to herself then said softly "you two have fun now." She made one sharp one hundred and eighty turn and sauntered out of the room, leaving me standing in the doorframe between her still startled and dismayed husband, standing pants down, next to the bed, and his lover, Ms. Coworker.

On our sixteen floor elevator ride, the housekeeper whistled gleefully. I stood next to her dumbfounded, rubbing my fingers through my hair, trying to appear cool headed, but I knew my face read absolute shock and confusion. Looking to the ground for redemption, I felt myself awkwardly coughing.

On the main floor, she turned to me, and in a dead quiet tone said, "I'll be leaving for my house now". Swallowing so hard my throat ached, I became her biggest cheerleader. "Well you know, do what you need

to do, and have yourself a great time," was the advice provided from the officer formerly trained in several forms of hand to hand defense combat, verbal judo, and negotiation techniques.

She smiled back at me. "I will"

The Honest John

Around seven P.M. on a Wednesday afternoon, I and two colleagues were dispatched to a noise complaint. We had received information that there may be a large number of people in the guest room, and that the loud music was disturbing most of the other occupants of the floor. We went expecting a perfect mid-day happy hour themed fiesta. The security manager, who had just finished dealing with a well-known celebrity guest's complaint's along with the hotel manager, had reached the room prior to arrival, and was waiting for us in front of the door.

We heard music blaring in the service elevator on our way up, but all things being equal, until we knocked on the door, it seemed as though it was going to be a completely standard noise complaint call.   A petite Hispanic lady answered our thumps on the guest room's door. She was fully nude spare a thong, with money strapped tightly into the string.

She carelessly and gleefully swung the door wide open, and stepped to the side so we could come in. Her invitation was cut short, however, when she looked to see who we were. When we made eye contact, she almost simultaneously attempted to slam the door shut, before we had a chance to speak. Another woman, also Hispanic, but wearing an oversized T-Shirt, grabbed the

door, before it closed to ask us, in a heavy accent, what we wanted.

Behind her were other naked and half clothed women, some mid-twenties, some desperately trying to make themselves appear to be mid-twenties, in a room full of partially clothed businessmen. Money had been thrown randomly all over the floor, and all the women were forcing themselves to act as if they were having the time of the lives. There were at least two couples actively having sex as we explained who we were and began entering the room to clear it of the occupants. It looked like a European red line sex club.

Upon our entrance, the girls magically started pulling clothes out of midair swiftly clothing themselves. The party seemed to immediately come to an abrupt end and the girls began pushing their way past us, making hasty escapes. Most chose to vacate the hotel completely. The security and hotel manager present for that day, decided not to pursue anyone leaving but to simply evict the party participants from the hotel, save for the recorded lodger.

The registered guest, of course, would be charged for whatever damages had occurred to the room. Consequently, we in the security staff cleared the room completely save the registered guest. He was an overweight, short, Caucasian man mid-forties. He was wearing an expensive gold watch and necklace, and it was very clear by his demeanor that he was somewhat affluent.

Much to the immediate shock of all present security staff members and the hotel manager, from an adjoining room, a man emerges; he was later discovered to be the brother of the registered guest. He was also overweight but was mid-thirties and had a few visible tattoos. He appeared to be the lesser accomplished sibling. Bottle dangling in one hand and slurring profanities, we assumed this man would be using all the liquid courage he recently acquired to be the resident tough guy.

Yelling at the fleeing women to come back to the room, the resident tough guy stated that the party wasn't stopping for anybody or anything until he had decided it would end. A few of the women momentarily paused to witness the final outcome, but most continued to make a beeline exit without so much as a second glance. Those that are smart enough to avoid penalties, often times do.

The two brothers quickly galvanized their efforts to be compensated for their pre-paid prostitutes and the services they hadn't fully received. The customer is always right, and by golly if we were going to stop the party, the hotel was liable. Therefore, they demanded compensation from the hotel.

When their ridiculous claim went unmet, the older brother became teary-eyed, and the other turned from his former tough man persona to begin to gently embrace and comfort his distraught brother. They decided, after discussing resolutions with each other in front of us, to sit on the floor in non-violent protest until

we met their demands. What type of so called fine establishment would refuse payment for prostitutes?

As hard as it was for me to keep a straight face, much less any resemblance of a stern face, I interrupted my manager to tell the brothers the hotel was not going to pay for the prostitutes, but if they would like we would get the police involved. The brothers could provide the police with the names of all those involved in the party, and the police could get in touch with the women to see if the women would return their funds. Elated, the men bound to their feet, ending their pitiful protest and demanded that we call the police. They insisted on not going anywhere until they spoke with a police officer. The few last remaining prostitutes took that as their cue to bolt toward all exits.

The police were called. The responding officer, when he arrived a few minutes later, stood quite literally dumbfounded as the brothers confessed without hesitation to hiring prostitutes. They said, they were good, honest, decent men, and they would not be swindled. They again made the claim that they would not be leaving the premise until their demands for repayment were met.

Looking the police officer squarely in the face, they again firmly demanded both he and his department locate the fleeing girls and either have them perform the duties which they were paid for or force the hotel to pay for their lost funds. If you believe yourself to be an honest businessman and keeper of funds, don't hire

prostitutes. As shocking a revelation as it may be, it's a fact that prostitutes do not follow standard business procedures.

Smiling ear to ear, the police officer briefly excused himself and called for his fellow officers assistance as well as a superior to be present as witnesses. This was mostly, as he told me later, because his comrades on the force would not believe his story unless they were there themselves to witness it.

Instantaneously, several police officers showed to provide assistance to a fellow police brother and began to methodically investigate the situation. The two brothers, embolden by the presence of a commander and several other police officers, in what they presumed to be a show of force on their behalf, repeated their prior confession as well as their demands.

Overcome with the absurdity of the scene, the first responding officer turned me, his face a shimmering plumb red trying to keep from laughing. His fellow officer began looking intensely into the ceiling lights to try in vain to hold back his amusement as the brothers threatened to sue the police department, the hotel, and all individuals present if their demands were not met. "He's not lying, my wife is an attorney, I'm giving her the full story, everyone here can consider themselves sued," the older brothers brazenly remarked.

With that closing threat, all bets were off. In a giant domino effect, we couldn't hold it in anymore. I had never before experienced such a deep belly laugh at

work.   One police officer, whom I worked closely with in the past, buried his head deep into my shoulder as he hooted, gripping me so he didn't fall from laughter. As I leaned into the wall, trying to bear his weight and hold on to my stomach, my sides began to ache.

Never before had anyone been laughed out of the building. The brothers, after our response attempted to march out indignant before they were arrested for soliciting sex and various property damage charges. They left in the back seat of a police cruiser, cursing at us.

From what I heard, from a later report, the man's wife, who was in fact an attorney, prior to divorcing him, represented the prostitutes pro bono.

Bleached

Not all opportunities for sexual intercourse are worth the cost of indulgence. Those working in the hotel industry must fight temptation when there are always empty rooms and beds available. Coworkers taking advantage of such open opportunities are not completely unheard of; however, the next story stands out in my memory as the most extraordinary.

One day, I found myself being dispatched to a room for both a medical emergency and a possibly violent disgruntled customer. When I arrived, I found a mother and two young male children standing in shock waiting outside of an uncleaned guest room. A perspiring housekeeping supervisor was bending over another female housekeeper who was on the ground, pants down, holding onto her exposed genitals, twisting in pain. Above the pair, stood a very angry father; he had a federal badge openly hanging by a chain around his neck, and a pistol in his shooting hand.

I found out that the father, who was a retired combat veteran and an active duty federal agent, was at the luxury hotel to celebrate his wedding anniversary with his family. When they checked in and came up to the room, he had heard loud noises, including cries and moans, coming from inside of his reserved room. He stated he initially believed someone was being injured behind the closed door.

Deciding to investigate the situation, prior to allowing his family to enter, he withdrew his pistol, and swiftly entered the room gun first to avoid any possible preparation for counter attack. Inside of the room, he discovered the terrified pair in the middle of love making. When the man, who the father would discover was a housekeeping supervisor at the hotel, turned to face the federal agent, there was a red laser pointed into his chest.

The supervisor fell off the woman and onto his knees with both hand lifted in surrender. After the agent commanded him to put on his pants, the supervisor pleaded with the agent not to kill them. Meanwhile, the agents' sons disobeyed their mother and peeped into the room to view the commotion and gasped in shock. The agent angrily shut the door and demanded the woman also find her clothes.

In a desperate attempt to hastily clean herself from her own sweat and the filth of the dirty bed, the woman grabbed the first cleaning bottle she could find and quickly sprayed her legs and genital region. Unfortunately, in her haste, she failed to observe that the bottle she grabbed was a bleach solvent.

She instantaneously crumpled to the ground in agony. Shooting and burning pains immediately traversed from the exposed veins and tissues of her genital region throughout her entire body. She fell to the floor, screaming in front of her distraught lover and the exasperated agent. The supervisor bent over his lover to

assist her as the military vet reached for the room's guest phone and furiously called the front desk to request immediate medical assistance.

The housekeeping supervisor told me that he and the housekeeper had decided to enjoy a bit of pleasure before business. Together they decided to take the risk of having sex and then to quickly clean the room together. They assured each other they could prepare and flip the room in the proper time frame allotted through a joint effort. However, they were so consumed by each other's passion, they lost track of the time. As both were married, the manager begged me to keep their tryst a secret.

Medically, this was a situation I was slightly unprepared for, and I felt as though there was not much that I could do to assist her. Though I had been thoroughly trained in first aid, this was not a situation for which training modules were created. I and a female coworker assisted her to the bathtub and began washing her genital region with warm water. Nonetheless, she suffered until the paramedics arrived to transport her to a local hospital.

As I looked that angry father in his eyes with his gun in hand, I wracked my brain for an adequate apology. He and his family had to endure catching my coworkers having sexual intercourse in a room reserved for them and then witness a housekeeper bleach her own vagina and be taken to the hospital. I sincerely questioned my loyalty to the company. I awkwardly

stumbled into an explanation of our compensation and reimbursement policy while the federal agent stood silently staring me down.

After speaking with the resort's senior management staff, we were able to provide the family with a complimentary upgraded room, a free dinner, and several free amenities. Nonetheless, as we gave them what we could, I could see by the agents' facial expression and body posture nothing could compensate what his family witnessed and the everlasting memory of housekeeper who bleached her own vagina.

Dumb To Dumbest

One night an engineering company, known for their revolutionary solar panels held a conference. The federal government at the time had dedicated a large portion of resources into funding the technological advancement of solar panel industrial equipment and several designers and engineers had rapidly found themselves flushed with cash. Notwithstanding the hotel's enormous size, the energy from their colorful displays and audio presentations reverberated throughout the ballrooms and onto the hotels' guest floors.

One of the individuals from the conference decided to order in a lady lover and told her to wait for him in the hotel's lobby. The conference attendees were encouraged to bring their families and few of the family members banded together and arranged to see the local attractions during their bread winners' meetings. The man allotted an hour after the business meetings were completed, while his wife was elsewhere, for his own personal enjoyment.

Due to the size of hotel, each of the guest floors had several wings. The rooms were numbered by both their location and the wing number. The man chose the room on the side closest to the convention area for his convenience in attending the occupational seminars.

His meetings concluded early and he went to his room to quickly stretch and prepare for his company. In a short period of time, the young woman called to say she was in the lobby and asked for his room number. When she received it, she took the first set of elevators to the designated floor. The woman, who came in wearing nothing but a large white trench coat and short red sundress, softly knocked on what she believed to be the room number. She then struck a seductive and revealing pose in front of the door.

The occupant, a middle aged business woman who was also returning from the same occupational meeting, was mortified when she opened the door to find the young woman standing provocatively in front of her. The prostitute, undeterred by the woman's surprise or the fact that a man had made the call for her, grabbed the business woman by the shoulder and whispered in her ear, "I'm the one you ordered baby." The mortified business woman, pushed her away, slammed the door and desperately called the front desk demanding security.

The prostitute's "real John," now irritated as his time was limited, left the room to find his mistress for the evening. Unbeknownst to him, she was standing in front of the wrong door, upset that the woman was not answering her calls. Frustrated at what she believed had been a waste of her time, she began yelling into the door trying to convince the woman to open the door and have relations with her.

Hearing a female's raised voice, the "john" goes down the corridor to investigate, hoping to assist the prostitute back to the proper location. By this time, the business woman was yelling at the front desk manager over the phone, venting her exasperation. She began packing her belongings, and angrily phoned down to announce that she would be leaving, and demanding a refund.

We arrive just as the prostitute and the business man meet and tenderly embrace. We hear the yelling of the professional woman, from the hallway, and knocked on her door to verify the identity of the prostitute who caused her the disturbance. Livid, she throws open the door, curses at us, the john, the prostitute and begins to leave with her belongings.

It took some time, but the front desk manager was able to convince her of the security and safety of the resort. He assured her that the individuals responsible would be properly dealt with and escorted out of the building. One of the security staff members accompanied the escort off the premises and myself and another guard walked with the man to retrieve his possessions from his guest room.

He had just finished packing his and his wife's belongings and was making his way down the guest corridor when he realized he would need an excuse as to why he had been removed and banned from even attending his previously scheduled meeting at the hotel. He came to the sudden conclusion that hiring a

prostitute, who happened to be not smart enough to go to the right door, was not the account he would like to relay to his wife.

Quickly, he turned, shouted an apology, then jumped and grabbed one of the floors overhead sprinklers. We rushed in immediately to stop him, but it was too late. As one of the guards grabbed him by the back, he lifted his legs, and propelled himself, sprinkler head in hand, downwards towards the floor.

Water from the pipes came pouring out of the ceiling. The first layer was covered in the dirt and the rust of the pipes. The pure density and quantity of water shocked the solar engineer. He lay on the floor as water soaked his belonging.

I desperately attempted to call engineering over the radio to immediately shut off the pipes but water had seeped into and destroyed the radio. Muddy water coated me, as I desperately attempted to dry off my personal cell phone to attempt to make the call. My efforts were to no avail, the avalanche of water effectively destroyed all electronic communication.

I could hear the frightened screams as guests rushed out of their rooms believing a fire was occurring on their floor. The fire sprinklers in the twelve surrounding rooms responded to their normal settings and activated. Panicking, the guests began to flee towards the elevators.

They were met there by the front desk manager. He had taken the initial business woman's safety into his own hands and was personally escorting her to her room, assuring her of the hotels security. When the two looked down the corridor, there I was fumbling with a useless radio while the man who had ordered the prostitute lay next to his floating belongings. The woman indignantly turned, slapped the manager in the face as he stood dumbfounded and followed the other floor guests in their retreat.

I have never seen a front desk manager curse the way he did. He cursed at the man who had caused the mishap, cursed at the pipes for the abundance of water they showered down, cursed the carpets for soaking up the water, and generally cursed at the fact that he had been made a fool. I attempted to calm him down, but it was to no avail.

Fortunately the sprinkler activation set off an emergency alarm. Engineers and additional security staff rushed in to investigate to assist and to shut off the pipes. But in the time the effort took, water had completely seeped through the flooring. As we escorted the man down the stairs to prepare to press damage related criminal charges, we saw water coming through the walls and falling onto the floors beneath us.

Not only did the man, destroy his own personal belongings and the luggage of nearly thirty other guests, but also damaged over sixty thousand dollars' worth of hotel flooring, walling, electronics and various other

properties. Despite his efforts to cover up his indiscretion, the truth came out in the lawsuit issued against him.

CHAPTER 2

Foolish Decisions

Prom

It's no secret proms can conclude in dramatic fashion. Teenagers find themselves temporally immersed in the emotional gulf of leaving behind the last bits of their childish womb, and, while pressuring themselves to be the coolest kid of the group, try to cram in as many memories as they can of friends whom they won't be spending their school days with anymore. While many see the end of their senior year as bright beginning, a final baby step before the leap to adulthood, the next story is of two teenagers who attempted to murder a cop and threw away their futures before they began.

Following a night where two proms by two different high schools were held in different ballrooms of the resort, my manager tells me to meet a police officer at a particular guest's room. He assures me he would be following me to the room shortly.

I ran into the police officer at the elevator bay. The police officer and I greet each other, and he informs me there is a distress call regarding a domestic fight in the guest room. He mentions that his partner will also be joining us and in route from another location.

As we approached the room, we heard three voices yelling, as well as loud knocks and other sounds indicating a fight in progress coming from inside of the guest's room. After knocking on the door, and providing

the proper notifications, I give the police officer the master key, and follow behind him as we enter the room.

Inside the room, two teenage boys are rolling on the floor, fighting. One taller boy was on his back, while a thicker, but stronger boy was on top of him, trying to apply some type of submission maneuver. Leaning against the far wall, a teenage girl is in the background pleading with the boys to stop fighting.

I and the police officer, after he commanded the two to separate, received their attention. The larger boy, after briefly glimpsing over his shoulder at us, jumped off the taller boy to his feet, and charged at us, head down, as we made our way towards the duo. He was quickly shoulder blocked to the ground by the officer.

The officer went down on one knee quickly turned the thicker boy to face a different direction than the other teenager. Calmly, he leaned in to administer handcuffs, talking the larger boy down as he did. From all appearance, it seemed at that moment, as if it would be normal high school fight, and that teenagers had just been caught up in their emotions.

The taller boy stood to his feet. He wiped blood from his nose with his shirts sleeves. Realizing that the attention was not on him, he seized the moment. Leaning over, he silently withdrew a pocket knife from a cabinet drawer. I looked over just in time to see him, arms formed into a windmill sweep, lunging at the police officer's exposed neck.

Inches from each other, I propelled myself fist first from the other direction, landing a picture perfect superman punch to the boy's unprotected jawline. I set my feet and prepared for a combination attack, but he collapsed instantaneously from the first punch. Dropping to his knees, as the ground gave out from underneath him, he falls awkwardly onto his back. His stiffened arms stretch into the air, and his eyes roll backwards. KO.

Only moments after saving the officer's life I quickly turned my attention to the young man. In order to eliminate the possibility of any permeant health concerns, I transformed myself from a combat hardened cage fighter into a male nurse.

Holding the boys head up and vexing his senses in an attempt to regain his consciousness, I called for the police officer, now kneeling no more than a foot away from me, to request an ambulance. The police officer radioed in the call, and then stands to assist me.

The thickset boy was still lying on his stomach; however, he had not been handcuffed and watched in traumatized silence as together I and the policer officer worked on restoring the taller lad's health and consciousness. The girl was still on the wall, now with two hands covering her open mouth, as she stood dazed in place.

Sensing he had been out shown and out done, the heavier lad, in an attempt to regain his role as the chief combatant in the room, grabbed the knife, from off of

the floor. He stood to his feet and we drew our attention from attending to the taller boy's health to focusing on him. With his demeanor and prior actions, he presented himself as a danger to our safety.

Immediately, as he saw the two of us prepare for his attack, he began to rethink his decision. Standing between the two other combatants, I saw from my peripheral the officer withdraw his Taser. Realizing he was outmatched, the boy chose flight over fight. Foregoing any attempt of further violence, he chose instead to make a beeline towards the door. Though he was now attempting to escape, we could not allow for him to do this either. He was still holding the knife, and due to his prior actions, we now considered him to be a potentially violent juvenile.

Almost at the door's threshold, the fleeing teenager was met there by my supervisor, a twenty two year Marine veteran. The officer yelled at the boy to stop running just as my supervisor gabbed the fleeing teen by the chest and arm attempting to control the knife in his hand. The larger boy, attempted to push my supervisor off of him, but his raw strength was no match the training and techniques the veteran was implementing.

Their struggle only lasted a brief moment. The police officer had already pulled the trigger and the prongs from the Taser connected with the large boys back. I heard my supervisor, the former Marine; emit a high pitch shriek as the electrical currents flowed

through both of the newly established opponents. The two collapsed together, arm in arm, onto floor.

The officer bellowed a resounding "SHITTT", and fumbled at his radio. The call was remade for two additional ambulances. I heard a shocked dispatcher ask quizzically, "You need three ambulances sir?" "YESS DAMIIITT" was the response she received.

We looked back momentarily to watch the girl, a petite, innocent looking teen.. She was wearing a mismatched combination of basketball shorts and a school football jacket. She stood mesmerized in the corner. With eyes larger than a UFO space ship, she raised both of her hands over her head in surrender regardless of any demand made to do so.

The officer hurdled over to assist the stunned pair just as his partner casually strolled through the door frame. He greeted, of course, by the scene of three hurt men laying on the ground. The taller boy slowly awoke to me, now tenderly attending to his health after I had, moments before assailed and knocked him out. The bigger boy and my supervisor lay stunned and twitching on the floor.

Once the ambulances arrive, and the boys' health were assessed. The knife was bagged for evidence, and the two teens were placed in handcuffs, before being escorted away. It was determined the boys should first visit the hospitable before being booked at the juvenile facility.

The young girl explained to us that she and the taller boy, a basketball player at her school, were a couple throughout the majority of their high school years. But on the very night of their prom, her true love betrayed her. He left her at the dance, and she saw him go off with another girl to a room. She suspected that he had been cheating on her with the other girl for some time. Disheartened and determined not to be alone for her prom night, she met and began chatting with a football player from the other high school who promised to console her. She invited him to her room.

After a long night of cheating on his girlfriend on their prom night, Mr. Basketball player returned to the room in order to retrieve his jersey and belongings, along with his girl, only to find Mr. Football in the room with his true love. After a brief heated verbal exchange, Mr. Basketball began swinging on Mr. Football. Mr. Basketball quickly found himself being spear tackled to the floor. Using some wrestling techniques which he had acquired while cross training, Mr. Football quickly gained the advantage in the fight.

Knowing her former love usually kept a knife with him, the young lady called the police. She stated she thought the boys would separate themselves when the police arrived and the matter would be amicably resolved.

Other prom attendees and friends of the kids involved jeered as the pair were brought in cuffs out to the ambulances awaiting them. The girl's parents were

called. With shame dripping from all of their non-verbal's, they were informed of their daughter's actions the previous night and informed she would have to appear in court. The only small consolation they received was that she had made the right decision to involve the authorities when she realized she could not handle the situation on her own. She would be considered a witness and not a participant.

Weak Arm Robber

Lost or reported stolen items are one of the more common occurrences law enforcement officials deal with when working at a luxury hotel. . Guests often find themselves in a relaxed state of mind, and care freely leaving their belonging unattended. For those unaware, the definition of strong arm robbery as defined by Justia.com is "offenses in which only personal weapons such as hands, arms, feet, fists, and teeth are employed or their use is threatened to deprive the victim of possessions." (I)

While criminality can sometimes forgo critical strategic planning and execution, there is only one thing a would be strong arm robber must remember before committing his offense; A strong arm robber should be more intimidating than the would be victim. In other words, if you want to pursue the life of a thief, and you see someone who is bigger than you, stronger than you, in short, generally more physically intimidating than you, and you're not armed or the world's paramount martial artist, don't try and rob them. This next tale serves as an example.

During a particular trade auction, featuring several competing vendors, we were called to come to the exhibition area for a fight between a retailer and an attendee. The call itself was somewhat unclear, when it came in, and it struck us as an odd call. Merchants

usually do not use violence as a modus operandi when attempting to create repeat customers. However, after rushing to the scene, we found the attendee on his back being smothered by the merchant.

The vendor was a very large Caucasian country boy. He was fully equipped with a torn Mountain Dew T-Shirt covering his beer gut. One of his sleeves had been cut completely off to expose an American flag tattoo covering most of his upper shoulder. The man's mud-stained jeans were buried deep into the much younger attendee's lower back.

The attendee, barely an adult, was a self-defined hipster. He had a sizeable gift product as well as his oversized non-prescription glasses lying next to him on the thin layer of carpet covering the concrete floor. His brown cargo shorts and green polo were receiving some organic dirt stains from the larger man's jeans and boots. A very unappreciative receiver, however, he was struggling, doing a sort of modified push up, attempting to turn from off his stomach in order to spit at the vendor.

After calming the situation down, and having the pair stand to speak with us, we quickly found out that the hipster had sauntered into the country boy's kiosk, declared that the vendor was selling garbage merchandise, knocked over a display tray with various trinkets, and then proceeded to grab a larger gift item from off the register counter. After telling the other customers to watch him, he had attempted to swagger

his way out from the kiosk. He had stated to some very surprised and disgusted onlookers that he would be walking out with the merchandise to end capitalistic tyranny of the shopkeeper.

When our vendor friend attempted to confront him, initially attempting to retrieve his item, the hipster, using his free hand, had attempted to push him away. While the mic wasn't dropped, the hipster was. The country boy, after a quick punch to attendee's jaw, tackled him, and held him face down till we arrived.

After the story that led up to our arrival was revealed, the vendor let the smart boy begin to provide his explanation, and found himself faced with a brigade of defensive rhetoric. The young man quickly turned from his role as tough guy activist, to the love child of two well experienced lawyers. He attempted to assure us that we did not need to provide any further assistance or investigation of the incident because his parents had instilled in him knowledge of legal precedence.

Despite his knowledge of the law, we explained to him that we needed him to come to the main security office, mostly so we could complete the necessary paperwork concerning the incident. We wanted to move him away from the crowd as to not disrupt the event any further.

Embolden by our politeness, he regained his prior strong male persona. Choosing me as his next target, he scowled at me, then turned and struck me with his fist as hard he could across my lower chest. He continued,

following up his punch with a heel kick to my ankle. He then quickly turned to run but found his pathway blocked by the vendor and my coworker.

After his initial spoiled child/my dad will solve my problems approach, I was more dumbfounded by his actions than physically hurt. I immediately grabbed the boy and swung him around to face off with him. "Well shit, that was a freaking bad idea" I heard the country boy mutter. The boy, stunned by my ability to recover after his attack, quickly realized I was a much stronger opponent than he realized.

While he began to stutter out his familial lineage, and again provide a detailed account of everyone in his family and their professions, I used the power of silence to answer his question about my authority. I stared directly in his eyes as I apprehended him by his elbow, but I was distracted by the perspiration commencing to form over his temple. Interrupting genealogical recital, I asked point blank why felt he could punch me and why he assaulted the retailer. He paused before answering. "Because I am an American citizen, and it is my right", he quizzically responded.

His response absolutely infuriated big guy behind me. I saw a flash of white lighting coming directly from behind my back. I quickly ducked as the country boy's All American fist again made the connection with the hipster's jawline. The hipster quickly dropped to a knee, shutting his mouth. He was quickly forced to realize that

he was in the wrong place to ignorantly speak ill of the rights of American citizens.

Insult a man goods, you'll upset him, try and take his goods, he'll make you pay, insult an American man's rights, and you'll attain his maximum fury. A hundred thieves could have completely dismantled the man's shop and taken it all away from him, the kid had the man's full attention.

My focus was now divided between keeping big man's bear sized paws behind me from destroying the hipster's very existence, and keeping the hipster moving away from his grasp. I began attempting to push the now volatile situation into the controlled area of the main security office. Pushing the hipster forward as he cowed in front of me, coworkers rushed in to assist me by protecting my rear. One guard cleared the way in front of us, as the vendor whose blood was boiling, followed behind cursing at the hipster. We followed my coworkers lead as we pushed them out of the exhibit hall and into the employee corridor towards our office.

We were met at our office by two police officers responding to calls from attendees about a fight. They were informed that we were in route to the office by the security manager. Our hipster, now conveyed himself to the police, not as a strong arm thief but as a consumer evangelist seeking to save the unknowing customer and everyday citizens from deceitful shop owners.

Just barely over the age of eighteen, it was determined by the responding officers to notify the

Hipsters parents prior to any decisions made by either party. The parents, who were in fact both successful lawyers, arrived and were absolutely mortified by their son's actions.

As the items were still in the vendor's custody, the parents attempted to offer a monetary contribution for the merchant's physical or mental sufferings, hoping to mediate any criminal charges. Their money was refused by the vendor, who stated he would rather press charges and attempt to receive justice through the courts than a monetary settlement. He was made aware and accepted the fact that he could face charges for the secondary punch he had thrown.

The young man was still arrested and convicted of attempted strong arm robbery. He was, however, offered a very generous plea deal, which many would argue was a direct result of his familial connections.

The Naked Man

It's a remarkably humid Thursday summer night. This particular weekend the resort was scheduled to host both a children's soccer and a youth cheerleading tournament. Although the events were being hosted by the same company, the tournaments were for separate sexes and hosted in different locations on the resort. The hotel received several modifications on the days leading up to the event. The changes had modified the hotel business convention hall into resembling a family friendly getaway.

Proud parents and family members brought their children from all over the nation to watch them participate in the countrywide competition. During the day, the company arranged for the children to either receive manicures at resident salons or to visit and explore the local attractions. The children were now set about preparing for a night of relaxation before the big competitions set for the proceeding day. Most of the parents were in the rooms with them, encouraging and supporting them.

One particular couple had just invited a cluster of their daughter's young friends and cheer mates to their king sized guest room. They had arranged with the other parents for a supervised girls sleep over. Expecting their company to be coming shortly, the couple had left their room door partially open.

Hearing the sounds of running in the hallway, the father begins to make his way towards the door to greet his children's friends and their parents. Just as he stands up, a man fully naked and carrying an ice bucket sprints past him and dives head first into the vending machine room located at the end of the hallway. The man nearly breaks the vending machine door and it swings wildly back and forth as he clumsily fumbles with the ice machine.

Mortified, the father loudly slams his door shut arousing the neighboring guests to peer through their peepholes. They too are greeted by the same naked man, ice now spilling from his bucket, speed walking his way back towards his room. Soon mortified gasps echo throughout the hallway.

I and another coworker were on schedule to watch the cameras, answer phones, and otherwise dispatch coworkers on calls as necessary throughout the night. A little past midnight, all three of our security phones began ringing simultaneously. We, of course, believing an emergency is unfolding are relieved to find it's only a naked man in the hallways; a call more common than you might imagine.

Finding out that he had indeed gone into a guest room, I quickly rewind the cameras on the floor's corridor to discover the room location. Keeping the cameras on the room and the guest corridor, I dispatch out two coworkers to speak to the man. One more coworker, a new hire, tags along for experience.

When the trio arrives at the room and knocks on the door, announcing their presence, the man still fully nude, casually strolls to the door to speak with my coworkers. As soon as my coworkers introduce themselves as security officers, the man falls to the floor and begins to attempt to roll himself away from the security officers. All the while, the man emits frightening giggles.

The camera perfectly shows the uncertainty going through all three of my coworker's faces as they debate between making an attempt to physically restrain the naked man or to find some other type of verbal restraint. As they process their options, the man, laughing, begins to gently bump into the security officers legs.

The newbie acts first and bends over to stop the man's rolls mid-cycle. The man pauses his roll to bend over, and the security guard is greeted with a shiny, hairy, buttocks staring back at him. He immediately throws his hands upwards, takes three steps back and turns away as if he had just stared directly into the mouth of a roaring flame.

As all three guards attempt to limit the irrational man's movement, without touching him, they stand together, force him to the door's precipices and block his pathway into the hallway. Suddenly, out of the room emerges a woman with bed sheet wrapped loosely around her skinny frame. The man stops his rolling and lays perfectly still, face up, laughing hysterically as the

woman covers him with towels. Stopping his laughs, he begins to scream in horror for ice to be brought to him.

The agents find out that the man is here, preparing to leave for his honeymoon. He had been married a few hours prior at a local church. His newly wed bride informed the agents that naturedly, he was a law abiding citizen and a bit of a square, however, she had convinced him to be bold and imaginary, and he had suggested using LSD for their wedding night.

Beyond any medical assistance we could provide for him, an ambulance was called. The man, sweating profusely and still acting illogically, he was strapped to a gurney and taken to the hospitable for treatment. The medics did stop by an ice machine, and allowed him to bring a cupful along with him as it seemingly calmed his fears.

Luckily for the groom, the hotel decided not to file a lawsuit against him, as many of the infuriated parents demanded to be compensated for the lewd disturbance during their stay. The parents did decide to file a civil suit and, although he had no recollection of the event, the amusing tapes provided enough evidence for a favorable resolution for the parents.

The Scared Tough Guy

One night, our dispatchers received a call from the hotel bar's manager, just before it was set to shut down for the night. The manager reported a disgruntled drunk customer and asked for assistance in removing him. Those of us who were called to respond were told that the man was upset because the bartender refused to serve him any more alcohol. After arguing with the barkeep staff, he attempted to go behind the bar to pour his own drinks.

Myself and one other female guard were first to arrive. We found the man to be in a quite casual demeanor. He was wearing colorful clothes and sitting on the sticky bar counter top; his feet were dangling off of the booth ledge, and he was singing in chorus with a pop song. Despite seeing the bar manager make the call for his removal, he seemed to be in a very personable mood.

We found out that the man was attending an international business convention. When we questioned him further to determine his identity, he suddenly decided he didn't speak English. We then asked how he was able to sing along with the song in English when we first arrived. After which, we discover he also acquired knowledge of several English profanities. He never lost

his smile; however, and he cursed at us while grinning ear to ear.

Fortunately for us, the bar manager was of the same ethnicity as the man and was able to speak to him in his native tongue. Immediately noticing that lack of knowledge was not an excuse he could use, he began to explain and to defend his actions in English. I smiled as he began talking, and he knowingly winked at me.

The bar audience was split in their opinion of the drunk. Half in the bar began to boo him and the other half, mostly those attending the convention with him, began to applaud him. He had become the shining star of his own evening show.

Nonetheless, we talked him off the bar counter and asked that he leave the bar and return to his room. Initially, we began to walk with him towards the door. I grabbed a water bottle and a Gatorade to assist him with his next morning's hangover. The crowd began to resume its normal chatter and laughter. The bartenders' service recommenced, and it appeared as if situation was handled.

Just as we reached the entrance of the bar, a young bar back began to leave the liquor room with the final fresh tray of various liquors. Surprisingly, in one quick moment, the man knocks over the bar back; jumps over him and into the liquor closet, pulls the door shut and attempts to barricade himself inside of the room. He takes boxes off of the shelves and pushes them against the glass door.

I angrily toss the drinks to the ground that I, in sympathy, retrieved for him. No more free drinks; no more Mr. Nice Guy. Having the master the key, I opened the door as the other guard focused on crowd control. I forcefully demanded that he leave the room and the establishment.

At this point, the drunken man decides to become momentarily irate. He again begins angrily swearing at me and tells me in no uncertain terms that he was "not going nowhere man, nooowwhhherrree." We tell him, either he is going to leave of his own accord, act reasonably, and go to his room, or we were going to call the police and he would be banned from the property including the convention he was attending. To be certain he understood, we asked the bar manager to translate the choices.

Faced with more aggressive options, he decides his best course of action is to start dancing. Grabbing bottles off the shelves, he employs them as shakers, and light heartedly begins to start singing for us, attempting to calm us down. He decided he would deescalate the situation through song and dance.

Incidentally, perhaps momentarily emotionally aroused, one of the ladies he had been flirting with at the bar, a taller local woman, walked over and stood behind us. She attempted to reason with him and asked him, in a sweet voice for him to kindly leave. He responded by throwing one of the glass bottles he had been shaking in her direction.

She squeaked and spun away hoping to avoid a collision with the glass, but the bottle hit the ground in front of her. The liquor and small shards of glass sprayed her face and summer dress. The man drunkenly laughed as the woman was quickly brought to the restroom by the female agent for a medical examination and to provide a written statement.

At this point, fellow convention attendees attempt to angrily persuade him to leave; hollering from the bar at him. He cursed out his peers. He again remained smiling. Many begin to encourage us to kick him out of the hotel and convention.

As we attempted to verbally pull him from the liquor room, he stopped his dancing. Hoping, I suppose, to impress us not only with his sense of rhythm but also by his physical strength. He began doing pushups on the room's concrete floor. The entire time, as lifted himself off of the floor, he stated, "call the cops, I ain't scared".

What the man didn't know was that the local police were already on the way to bar to retrieve their nightly left over fries, chicken tenders, mozzarella sticks, pizza slices, burger sliders, etc. In return for complimentarily receiving the bars nightly left over's, they traditionally assisted us with any disorderly guests. The bar manager stepped outside to make the phone call for their assistance just as they were coming through the door. They greeted as usual, then he informed them their late night usual dinner plans would temporally have to be

placed on hold, and that I was in the middle of dealing with a situation.

Frustrated, they came over hoping to quickly remove the man, and resume their nightly ritual. As soon as the man came to the realization that the police were indeed here for his removal, he broke down crying. His entire tough guy persona immediately faded. Suddenly he did care if the police came, and he transformed himself into a pitiable man. He stopped his pushups, laid on his stomach, and began to cry.

The woman, still wet with alcohol from her encounter with him, came out of the restroom to see him crying on the floor. We told the officers of his attempted assault, and he got on his knees to beg her for her forgiveness. Tears streaming down his face, he sobbed his apology. The immediate transformation was too much for the woman, and she began laughing at him. He embodied all of the charisma, musical talent, comedy, and drama befitting of any late-night show. Despite her prior anger, he thoroughly amused her.

He paid for the bottle he broke, and no charges were administered. He was rewarded, after such an awesome spectacle presentation, with a simple forced escort off of the property. Bellmen were sent to retrieve his belongings as he waited in a cab to be driven away.

Fighting a Helping Hand

It's the night of New Year's Eve. The hotel was being rented by a private contractor throwing a lavish New Year party. Tickets and hotel registration were priced extravagantly, however, there was an open happy hour bar, a light show, a champagne waterfall, a seafood buffet, a scheduled ball drop, and a late night dance in the main ballroom. Attendees took full advantage of the complimentary amenities provided throughout the evening.

I and my coworkers working the night shift arrived to work fully expecting drunken disorderly guests, fights, and more than the usual unsanctioned guest room parties occurring in the guest rooms and corridors throughout the night. Knowing the difficulty the night would hold, the hotel offered its graveyard shift employees a pay incentive for working the night.

Soon enough, an agent on patrol calls for any available security agents to meet with him at on the highest floor in the farthest stairwell. The stairwell itself ended with two perpendicular doors. One door led to an elevator shaft, the other to the roof of the hotel. Myself and another colleague were first to respond at the scene to assist our coworker.

Upon our arrival, we witnessed a man acting irrational. He was in his early thirties, Caucasian, slightly balding, and extremely thin. The first security guard was

watching as the man who was laughing and sweating excessively, ran up and down the one flight of stairs. The man kept repeating his actions: reaching a landing and turning and running either back up or down the stairwell.

The man informed all of three security agents now present that he believed he was led into the stairwell by ghosts as part of a video game. He said it was his first time playing this game, but he recognized he would be playing it until he died. It was very clear that the man was hallucinating and had probably had consumed narcotics. We attempted to figure out which he had consumed in order to determine how best to assist him.

When we stood in front of him, and tried to attain some basic information from the man, he outright refused to talk to us about anything other than the game he believed he was playing. The more we tried to talk to him, the more confused he became. Somehow, he convinced himself that we were referees for the game and we presented ourselves to assist him follow the rules of the contest.

The contractor had hired additional private security and medical staff for the night, and we had provided them radios. They were informed of the situation and, after some initial confusion in regards to the location, they arrived to help us with Mr. Hallucinations. The man was reluctantly transported to the main medical room set up by the hotel for the event.

While we were there, the man sobered up briefly and informed us that he had a brother. His brother was

identified as a guest staying in the hotel. After a brief call to the room, we were able to locate the brother. We were told the man was staying in his brother's room for the night, and he was probably under the influence of PCP.

The other brother, younger by three years, and an extremely well built personal fitness trainer, took some time in making his way to the medical room. When he did appear to claim the Mr. Hallucinations, we strongly suggested bringing the man to the hospitable for the night. His brother, fully sober, refused as he stated his brother's health care was through his brother's job. The trainer believed the insurance company would be obligated to report medical situations as a result of his illegal activities to his brother's employer.

The younger brother stated his brother often took PCP and wanted the man to sleep off the drugs as he had witnessed his brother do several times before in the past. It appeared as if older brother had regained nearly full consciousness, so we were able to walk him back to his sibling's guest room.

After the embarrassing assisted walk to the guest room, we informed the befuddled older brother that he should remain in his younger brother's room for his own safety, the remainder of the night. The trainer demanded his brother to attempt to sleep off his hallucinations. He half nodded in agreement. Feeling unable to lift his heavy head, he collapsed into the bed's comforters.

About forty five minutes later, another security guard, who was in the ballroom ad previously not

involved in the first incident, came across the brothers in the midst of a heated argument. They were directly in the middle of the party and partiers had stopped the dance floor to watch the two scream at each other.

Thinking his brother had gone to sleep, the younger brother returned to enjoy the celebration with his friends. In middle of his dancing, his brother randomly wandered into the party in a confused state. When the younger brother asked why he was there and not even attempting to recover, the older brother began to stutter about an imaginary game. The event security was present and engaged the situation prior to us coming.

As the two began to get louder, one of the surrounding men, watching the situation unfold with drink in hand but still attempting to dance with his lady, slipped and fell to the floor. His drink happened to land on the older brother shirt. His girl began to laugh at the dancer's fall. When the dancer got to his feet and began to apologize, the older brother ripped off his own shirt and began pounding on his chest with balled fists. With strength I can only attribute to the drugs in his system; he used one hand to push his younger and stronger brother into us as we approached the pair. He resumed pounding his exposed chest and shouting over the noise of the crowd and music, "I am a champion, I am a heathen."

He hit himself until his chest was nearly fully discolored. The veins on his neck bulged, his teeth

clenched, his eyes, though initially expanded, became watery from the burning pain. In the midst of absolute fury, he attempted stare down any one, man or woman, who would dare to meet his gaze.

After initially politely asking him to leave, he turned and struck one of us. We grabbed him by the shoulders and waist and pulled him out of the party. His brother stood behind us, and held the remains of his brother's shirt, as we forcibly removed him, before he potentially struck or hurt anyone else.

The police department was notified and arrived approximately fifteen minute later to assist. When the older brother again refused to vacate the property he was forced to leave under the authority of police. He was placed under arrest for disorderly conduct and criminal trespass. Unyielding, he cursed at any individual he saw witnessing his arrest process.

Once in the police car, he began to realize his error. He began to apologize to us, the police, his younger brother, and the audience member who were watching him. But it was too little too late for him. His brother didn't want to hear his apology or his cries for sympathy. He had driven six hours to party, paid for the room, offered him a place to stay for free, paid for their tickets, stood by his side when the drugs had forced him into irrational behavior, and had remained by him while he received medical assistance. He was done. He tapped on the top the cruiser and told his brother to get

sober. He then walked back inside to join his friends in enjoying their night.

The older brother sobbed and kicked at the door of the cruiser in an ineffective attempt to free himself as he was taken to jail for the night.

CHAPTER 3

Evil Deeds

The Pedophile

The long exhaustive day was finally drawing to an end. The mother and father, both professionals in the same industry, were at our lavish hotel attending a convention filled with conference meetings. Various industry experts and motivational speakers had presented throughout the early morning and into the evening. The couple spent the majority of their day in meetings, and, at the same time, networking with other ambitious and overly friendly wealth chasers. Their oldest son, a barely twenty one year old college sophomore, had been dragged along to watch their youngest child, an eleven year old girl they adopted from Vietnam as an infant.

Wearied from their day, the mother, father and son decided to catch a quick late afternoon drink at a local bar, while the daughter, whom they left behind was told to stay in the room. The father left his cellphone with the daughter, telling her to call him if she needed assistance. As the three socialized, what began as a solitary happy hour turned into an evening out. They believed their daughter would stay in their room and be safe until their return.

Left alone, their daughter became bored and decided to find another way to enjoy herself. Somewhere during the evening, the young girl went to the pool. Thankfully, however, she texted her mother, from her father's cell phone, letting her know of her whereabouts.

True predators never prematurely reveal themselves, as it will scare away their prey. They wait patiently, drawing closer and closer, for the opportune moment to strike.

Alone at the pool, the child was approached by one of her father's coworkers. He didn't offer her candy, or video games, or anything remotely childish; he treated her the way he imagined she wanted to be treated. Witnesses later stated he remarked on how grown up she looked and how she was blossoming into a young adult.

He had identified from his interactions with her at her parent's office that she was at developing state which was beyond the simplistic desires of a small child and she desired to be loved in a mature manner, similar to her parents. She wanted to be an adult, and he pretended to treat her like she was one. He asked her to his room for drinks and conversation, and she innocently followed his lead.

Sometime later that evening, I was dispatched to the room. Another guest, directly across the hall, was disturbed when she heard loud screaming and crying coming from the room. Upon my arrival at the scene, I heard the whimpering of a child as well as the steady creaking of a bed frame and heavy male grunts.

I felt a gut sense of impeding danger, and I immediately called for a supervisor to assist me with addressing the situation. As the concerned middle aged female guest stood in her door frame and timidly

watched, I hammered at the door and as loudly as I could scream I identified myself as hotel security.

My louds knocks clearly startled the occupants of the room. I immediately heard the bed creak as if a large weight had been removed. A brief female groan of pain, and the sounds of footprints approaching the door followed. A middle aged man, fully clothed in business casual attire saves for his shoes and belt, hurriedly answered the door.

He stood in the door frame constantly avoiding my gaze. His eyes quickly darted back into the room. Swinging his hands horizontally and rubbing them together as he talked, he immediately began to talk charmingly to myself and the other guest watching and his intentions immediately became apparent. He was seeking to avoid any further investigation.

In the midst of his talking, the young child walked over to see what was going on. She struggled to stand as her small knees trembled and she quickly moved to lean against the wall for support. She was fully naked. Her eyes displayed her horror as she looked up into the man's darting gazes back to her. I could see blood streaming down her legs and tears in her eyes. She was trying to catch her breath, still not understanding fully what had happened, or what was now happening. I heard from behind me the lady gasp, "oh my lord" as her door was slammed shut.

My superior arrived at the guest room. The man stopped talking. He stopped rubbing his hands together

and grabbed for a glass of alcohol on the dresser. The supervisor closed the door to protect the child's privacy and followed me into the room. As we cross the door's threshold, the girl jumped into the bed, and innocently hid herself under the comforters for protection.

A call for police assistance was made by my supervisor as the situation turned violent. The man initially yelled fatal threats, attempting to intimidate myself and my supervisor; however, when the verbal forewarnings went unheeded, the man swung at me with a glass bottle. I was now being attacked with what I could reasonably presume to be with malicious intent with a dangerous weapon.

Wildly swinging, the bottle was smashed against a wall and spraying glass shards shredded their way into my shoulder. Using the last large unbroken portion of glass, the man lunged at me, cutting me on my elbow as I extended it to block my neck and head. Keeping my bloody arm still close to my neck, without any further hesitation, using my free hand, I pulled my pepper spray from my belt and sprayed the man's face.

While he gripped his burning face and eyes, gasping for air, I tackled him. I put my knee in his chest and began bashing in his nose and mouth with my fists. The bottle shards covered the floor around us, and he grabbed them. Bloodying his own hand, he made a fist full of glass shards. With all his might, he attempted to punch the glass into my stomach and chest.

I heard the girl in the background. Underneath the protection of the bed covers, she wasn't screaming or whimpering; she was sobbing, no longer from the physical pain but from the shock of the sexual assault. Her cries captured my attention, and I stopped for a brief moment to clear the tears in my own eyes. They were not from the effects of the pepper spray, or the pain in my now bloody arm, chin, chest, stomach, and shoulder, but from the realization of what happened to this young girl.

I continued punching him; this time harder than before. Not only had he attacked me forcefully with a weapon to do serious bodily harm but he had caused injury to my person. My supervisor, awaiting the arrival of the police watched from the doorframe to make sure it was a fair contest.

When the police arrived, my head was clear, and I remained completely silent refusing to provide an account, as my supervisor explained the situation. Nothing much needed to be said. The girl lay in the bed, blood covering her legs and the sheets; the pillows soaked with her tears. My blood covered my arm, chin, stomach, chest, and shoulder and there was a broken bottle with glass shards inside of my skin. The man's face was bruised and bloodied, and he displayed evidence of the residuals from the pepper spray.

Paramedics were called to address the wounds of all involved parties. The girl was immediately transported by ambulance to the nearest hospital. While two of the

paramedics, who had come for the young girl stayed behind to address our wounds. They administered first aid until more paramedics arrived. Both the pedophile and I were transported to the emergency room.

The police used as much force as they could to justify the arrest process. When we were initially separated, the pedophile had attempted to use the bottle as weapon against the police. Not only was he tazed, pepper sprayed was again administered. Perhaps the only reason he did not find himself killed was the child was in the line of fire, hiding herself underneath the sheets. Moments like these break the best of men and the police officers found themselves to be of no exception. Once on the ground, his face was held next to the broken the glass shards he had used to attack me as his handcuffs were administered.

As I watched his arrest process unfold from the ground, paramedics treating my wounds, I saw the police throw a towel over his now bruised and bloodied face. As both myself, now clothed by bloody wraps and without any uniform, and the cuffed wounded pedophile were walked out the hotel by the police officers towards the awaiting ambulances, I heard the chant of police brutality screamed from unsuspecting bystanders.

In my own opinion, the man deserved every bit of the beating he had just received from both me and the police. But the police couldn't tell the bystanders the truth of what occurred. For his own protection and to ensure due process, the police officers morally and

legally could not share the pedophiles crimes. They could only be polite to those criticizing our actions and ask that they calm down.

The girl had left the cell phone in the man's room, and in her emotional state, was not able to provide us any information besides her parents' names. Using information on the phone as well as data provided by the guest registration, the investigators were able to track down the parents to attain a complete account of everything that transpired. From the time which the text sent, via camera surveillance, we were able to capture the man's interactions with the child completely from start to finish and identify witnesses.

Domestic Murder

There must be nothing more pleasant in this life as waking up in comfortable bed, expensive amenities thrown care freely around a room someone cleaned for you, free from all employment and social obligations, hearing the sounds of birds witlessly singing their bright morning songs, as your boyfriends fist slams into you intestines. You instantly realize as you wake from the night's sweet release of reality, your morning routine will now include an extra layer of foundation, as the initial fist to the guts is followed by a slap across the face. You roll off the comforter to the plushy carpeted floor, to escape another jab, but are followed down by your love. Nearly on the floor, feet still propped onto the bed, you struggle to breathe, as he ground his muscular hands into your throat, furiously staring you down as he comes.

One early morning, simultaneous to our shift change and us clocking in, we received information from disturbed guests that there was a domestic fight occurring in one of the luxury suites. No time for the cheap morning coffee in a cheaper Styrofoam cup, no time to greet your coworkers and shake off the morning cobwebs; hello, good morning, welcome to your job, now go stop an impassioned domestic fight.

I and a female coworker arrived first. We heard the low female pants and a barely audible woman's voice, begging a man to get off of her. The man was speaking

in a foreign language, but we were unable to discern the situation, if there were weapons present, if they were being used or what amount of force was being used.

The noise stopped suddenly as the only sounds became loud breathing. Unsure of what we heading into, the decision was made to request police assistance. After a minute of terrible silence, and unsure if the woman was conscious or even alive, we knocked on the door and announced our presence. After three attempts without a response, we quickly used the master key and engaged the room.

The woman, Arabian, was on the bed, shirtless and face up, softly panting, clearly out of breath, tears in hers and bruises on her face, arms, throat, and stomach. Fist sized holes covered the wooden head rest above her. The man, Caucasian, also shirtless with military tattoos covering his arms and body was sitting in the chair facing us, calmly and patiently awaiting our entrance. With his left hand, he was gingerly rubbing his bloodied right hand. He had covered it with a wet toilette, but it was obvious he would need far more medical support.

Despite the small distance separating them, and the woman's frightened gaze in his direction, the man did not show the slightest concern for the woman. He completely and un-hesitantly complied with the command to remain seated and to place his hands on top of his head. He answered only questions about his personal information, but remained completely unbothered by his own actions and unconcerned about

the potential consequences. His only request was that we administer first aid and sanitize his hands, specifically, his right fist.

There was never a reason presented by the man for the assault. We found out he was in fact in the military and had met his girlfriend while being deployed overseas. She was of Saudi Arabian descent but was born and raised as a citizen of France. When they met, she was in the Middle East assisting with humanitarian aid and was in the in the military. After several months of being together overseas, he was bringing her home to introduce her to his family and friends.

The woman was taken inside the restroom with the female guard to address and remedy her bruises and lacerations and also to get dressed. Although she informed us that he had attacked her, punching and choking her for no apparent reason, she was quite adamant that she did not want the police involved. When they did arrive, as we had made the call prior to engaging the situation, she absolutely refused to provide a statement against her man, any of the assistance they offered, or to press any type of charges.

Both the police and ourselves attempted to reason with her, and shared examples of incidents occurring in the past which we had dealt with, but she refused our help. Though she did listen to our stories, she told us, her own father was a French police officer, and she stated she had witnessed her parents overcome domestic

difficulties. She was confident her own relationship was worth more than this incident of abuse.

The destruction of hotel property, however, was sufficient enough for the hotel and the police to press charges on the man. Although he denied the accusations, and the woman attempted to retract her previous statements, the wood splinters from the room were found embedded into his right fist. The holes in the bedframe were also similar and the exact size of his fists.

His arrest upset the woman. She pleaded for his release as handcuffs were administered. She did not want to interrupt the family plans the couple had previously scheduled. It was obvious why he was unconcerned in regards to his assault on her. He knew she would not let go of him. We found ourselves having to convince her that she did not need to blame herself for his actions.

Those willing to hurt you, will, if you allow them the opportunity. After the charges were filed and bond posted, the man went to a family members house, attained a .38 357 magnum revolver from that family member and returned to the hotel the next day around three in the morning.

Knocking on the door of his unsuspecting girlfriend, he resumed where had previously left off hurting her, when she had opened the door, shooting her twice in the abdomen. He had then turned and coolly walked away leaving her bleeding, crying and clutching her stomach in the door frame.

Our security team, pulled up the cameras and immediately responded. They rushed to the scene and wrapped her stomach, in an attempt to minimalize the loss of blood. The bullets themselves were lodged deep in her abdomen; however, they discovered most of the bleeding to be internal. An ambulance was called, and she was rushed to the hospital, but despite all efforts, she was pronounced dead approximately six hours later.

As he was in the hallway at the time of the shooting, the entire crime was caught by our video surveillance system. Although, he later attested in court that he was looking to injure her, the shots landed in her spleen and liver. The poisons released had led her to die in excoriating pain. The man later provided a confession and accepted a plea deal. No motives, if any even existed, were ever established

I returned to the hotel four hours after the shooting, again working the morning shift, and stood outside the door. My objective was to deter guest entry or interference, as detectives and crime scene investigators analyzed and dismantled the room to gather all necessary evidence for prosecution. Again, later that day, I was called in to assist as a specialized police recommended unit, cleaned the blood from the wood of the door, and stripped away the wall paper and carpeting of the room so that they could properly be replaced.

One bright early morning, I had warned the woman not to allow the man to take advantage of her desires for love and natural purity of heart. The next

morning, I watched as her blood and guts were removed from the room. The lesson of this story is simple cold truth; pillagers do not care about the feelings of those that they mistreat. There are people who will hurt you, despite your best intentions, if you give them the opportunity.

The Final Party

Parties are common occurrences in the hotel industry. Due to the pure size of the hotel, we often expected at least three parties per weekend. While some affluent individuals choose to notify the hotel and arrange elaborate festivities for themselves and their acquaintances, unplanned or unsanctioned room parties are much more common.

This story begins with an alcohol fueled fraternity party occurred in a presidential suite on the top floor. The room was nearly seventeen stories above ground, and was often booked for both its luxury and view of the surrounding city. The presidential suite came with a partially stocked bar, chandelier, wooden floors, lavish tapestry, a floor to ceiling window in its kitchen and an external balcony in its rear dining hall.

After numerous complaints of cigarette smoking, and various other room infractions, as well as two prior negative interactions with the registered guest, we were sent to facilitate the conclusion of the party. As we had previously observed several individuals in the room, five of us initially responded to assist in the parties' interruption.

As we made our arrival a third time to the guest floor, littered plastic cups provided a pathway through the guest corridor to the room. There were several young adults both inside and outside of the room, most of

whom were thoroughly inebriated. They were conversing and dancing as strobe lights replaced the usually glow of the room, and hypnotic-trance music was blaring through brought in speakers. A few had taken to the balcony to smoke.

We made our usual announcement and began to disperse the crowd. There were dismayed outcries and drunken pleas but when the music was shut off, and lights turned back on, most found their way to the door. A few of resorted to calling us various names, but nothing truly seemed out of the ordinary. Most of the younger party goers, mostly female teens, were the first to leave especially since they were underage and drinking.

As we made our way to the back of the apartment and the balcony, we saw several extremely intoxicated underage teens. These teens were unaware that we had arrived to end the party. We made our way through the departing crowd, over to them to make sure they understood the party was being shut down and to check on their physical health. We could see vomit on the floor close to where they were standing and their lack of experience drinking was absolutely and undeniably visible.

As we approached, we startled one of the teen girls. She was barely standing, scarcely holding a cheap bottle of vodka, slumping against one of her female friends. We later learned she was a freshman and this was one of her first college parties.

In one terrifying moment, we watched as the teen looked up, realized who we were and panic. In a desperate attempt to not be caught in possession of alcohol, she threw her bottle through the opened balcony doors. The bottle barely missed a young man, who ducked to miss impact, and it sailed past him off of the verandah.

Pushing the students out of way, we rushed to gaze beneath the deck. A horrifying view met our stares. We saw a lady in her mid-forties, lying motionless on the street. She had a long evening coat on, and bags laying on the concrete next to her.Even from our distance, we spotted the pool of blood surrounding her small frame.

Time paused for a horrifying moment. I saw, the partygoer who had just ducked, hands go limp. He dropped his cigarette over the balcony, and covered his chest in terror as he stared down. Whether it was the pure vertical distance, the annihilation that lay beneath him, or the realization of the possibility the personal peril he had just avoided, I will never know, but he stood perfectly still and speechless, unable to gaze away.

Turning, we saw the girl fall sloppily into a drunken stupor onto the couch as her friends laughed at her. They were completely oblivious to the sobering scene beneath them. Everyone on the balcony, who had seen her throw the bottle, knew the drunk teenage girl had inadvertently killed a woman to hide her drinking.

Other security officers, not assisting with the close of the party, were sent to help the lady. They rushed over

with bandages, and did what they could to cleanse and close her lacerations. They held her head up, made a desperate attempt to stop the blood rushing from her temple. As her eyes were initially opened when they arrived, they attempted to speak with her, but she was unable to speak. She briefly forced herself to look in the directions of the guards, but blood sprouted from mouth when she attempted to respond.

A desperate call for an ambulance was made. Despite their arrival less than seven minutes from the time of the call, the action of the professional care givers proved to be futile. The glass bottle had landed on the ladies head. The skull was fractured, and her neck had been twisted and splintered from the impact. It was a needless waste of life caused by the lack of judgment of a drunken teenager.

Unfortunately, not only was the life of the woman who died wasted, the lives of those attending the party that nights were permanently disrupted. The early twenties man who had reserved the room and several of his friends were charged with providing alcohol to minors, along with various other charges. The fraternity was banned from existence at its university. The young ladies friends were charged as accomplices, and the teenager girl was arrested for involuntary manslaughter, reckless endangerment, and various other charges. A brief moment of panic led to the tragic and needless ruin of several lives.

Sister Kidnapper

The constant encumbrance of living with and supporting a family member suffering from mental illness can bring about regrettable moments of distrust and unconcern. When moments of erratic and violent behavior erupt, instantaneous emotionally charged reactions sometimes do occur. Unfortunately, often times, the individual suffering will not fully comprehend their own actions or the reactions of other family members and there are times where the mental illness can stimulate feelings of betrayal and rage.

On the very tail end of what had been a remarkably quiet weekend night, while struggling to push through the groggy last two hours of the dreaded weekend graveyard shift, I stepped outside for a refreshing breath of the night air and to watch the city awake. The autumn air was cool and crisp, and dew rested on the fallen leaves.

Directly to my left, I see two tall teenage girls sitting on a bench, and above them stood a slightly younger teenage boy who was at least six feet five inches tall. Though he was tall, the boy looked infirm. The situation seemed odd, as the young man paced back and forth in front of the girls switching between excitedly shouting and whispering. I saw panic in the eyes of the girls. When they saw me in uniform, they waved for me to come over and to assist them.

As I approached, I saw in the boy's eyes a kaleidoscope of emotions and mental uncertainty. He initially stopped his pacing to glare at me over his right shoulder as I approached. Unsure of my motives, he turned his body to face me, and I could see in his left hand, he was clutching onto long switchblade. The blades metal reflected off a lamppost's light. Its light was shining at me against the backdrop of the dark moonlight.

Keeping him in my view, I paused to quietly radio for back up. Still approaching, I grabbed his full attention, and the girls, both taller than me, scurried behind me towards the hotel's entrance. Initially, the boy waved the knife in our direction and screamed incoherent phrases. I felt a sense of urgency to protect the young girls behind me, and, when he saw I would not be deterred, he walked threateningly toward me.

As he got within a foot of me, I started to prepare to defend myself. He suddenly stopped, turned so his back was facing me and started to yell into the night air. I asked him what was bothering him and how I could help him and attempted to offer a reasonable resolution. When he attempted to respond to my offers, nothing he said was a fully developed thought.

He seemed to have trouble not only expressing himself, but also with his thought process. At one point, he claimed he was being controlled by a secret government agency and his mission was to be bigger

than any movie star. He then switched his story to say that he was a misguided youth who just desired to be loved by a family who hated him. He said he had never felt truly loved.

I began to attempt to motivate a positive and impactful resolution and to ask why he felt so negatively. Instead of answering verbally, he turned and pulled the knife to his own throat. He stood there silently, staring at my mortified expression. I contemplated the words I needed to convince him to spare his own life when the girls rushed from the entrance, yelling at him to stop.

One of them quickly identified themselves to me as his sister. Together they briefly shared that he was both mentally challenged and had been using hard drugs the previous evening. Finding himself unable to sleep, he tossed and turned throughout the night, troubled by his own thoughts.

During the night, he began thinking about how his mother loved his sisters more than she loved him. He quietly woke his sisters, directed them outside the hotel and told them his only option was to kill them to receive the totality of his mother's love.

Thinking how he had a much longer reach than me, was mentally unstable and a minor, the best course of action was for to not to physically engage him. His troubles were mental, so I attempted to bring him back to a measure of sanity.

Other coworkers arrived to assist, but stood behind me, as I was already verbally engaging the situation, waiting, if necessary, to jump in for physical confrontation. One guard called for police assistance as I continued in the de-escalation process. When I asked him why he would arrive at the conclusion that killing his own sisters would bring about his mother's love, he slowly turned in a full circle, talking incoherently while dropping the knife and laying on his stomach down on the bench.

I sent his sisters to the mother's room to retrieve her, hoping that she would be able to de-escalate the situation further.   Awakened at nearly five in the morning with the news that her son had forced his sisters out of the room to publicly kill them, she sprinted down the stairs to find her son who was now surrounded by three security guards, and four police officers lying on his stomach, still on the bench, unhand-cuffed, and silently staring at his pocket knife.

Surprisingly, the mother barely stood just over five feet tall, but she made up for physical lack in size by a possessing a commanding attitude. After assessing the situation, she didn't show any compassion. Her first words were directed towards the police. She demanded that her son be placed under arrest and dragged off in handcuffs. Looking her mentally challenged son in his eyes, she angrily voiced that she wanted him to get beaten and raped in jail. She believed it would put the fear of authority in his heart.

The passive environment I had successfully created prior to her "assistance" was shattered. His initial imaginations now renewed by his mother's cold demeanor, the boy's mind snapped. He shouted as he was placed under arrest how he should never have waited, and that he should have killed his sisters in the room in front of their mother. He didn't think his mother deserved any children and he again became incoherent, rambling to himself.

After he was forcibly removed, the mother, seemingly unconcerned, told the daughters, "C'Mon if you're coming back up, I'm going back to bed". The daughters were absolutely devastated by both the evilness and cruelty in their mother's lack of empathy towards them or her son. Together, holding hands, they followed their mother up to the room.

Pizza Murder

It was an early summer night. Graduation season was coming to a close and we found ourselves nightly closing down graduation parties. Alcohol freely flowed as graduates celebrated the culmination of years of hard work and achievement.

Each guest room has a guest phone, which among many other services, has a bright red emergency button. When pushed, the button rings to special phone in our office with a very distinct ringtone. The room number was displayed on the front of the phone when it rang and it was set up in such a way that if we did not pick up the phone in a minute time frame, the call would be immediately transferred to the police.

Due to the sheer size of the facility, and the amount of calls received, emergency or otherwise, it was mandatory for at least two people be present in the dispatch office at all times although three to four individuals usually manned the station. Training for this position requires a two week course, and the office is usually filled by senior staff members.

In the middle of the night, while giving one of the scheduled dispatcher's a fifteen minute smoke break, I received a call on the emergency line. On the other end, the caller, a crying female, asked that I send some help to her guest room. She stated her brother was being violent and acting crazed.

I dispatched three available security agents to the room. When the second scheduled dispatcher returned a few minutes later, personally went with the night manager to join my coworkers at the room. By the time we arrived, the other coworkers had already engaged the situation.

When they had knocked, an older European American lady, answered and was asked them to step outside to speak to them. The woman's appearance was in disarray, her clothes wrinkled, and she was sweaty. She attempted to explain the situation prior to the security officers going inside, but her explanation were interrupted when the sound of two men shouting at each other was heard coming from inside of the room. They had been asked to join in on the volatile situation with no knowledge of its origin.

By the time the night supervisor and I became present, security staff were inside the room asking questions to determine a resolution. An older thickset man, identified to be the woman's brother, was shouting in a heavy Italian accent at both the security staff and a shorter balding Caucasian American man, identified to be the woman's boyfriend.

The brother was pacing the room in front of us, and we could smell alcohol on his clothes and breathe. The room, itself was a double queen and there were damages which displayed signs of a struggle. One of the mattresses had been pushed off of the bed, the glass on one of the counter tops was cracked, and a lamp lay

broken on the floor. Some of the suitcases had been thrown against the front wall.

When we asked our initial questions, we discovered the woman, had recently graduated with her doctorate. She had moved to the United States at eighteen, and had spent her last twenty years in the States pursuing a medical career. Her brother had come from Italy, and together, along with the woman friends and colleagues, they were at the resort for the weekend celebrating the occasion.

The couple and the brother had gone to a bar directly across from the hotel where the sister had introduced her brother to some of her friends. After a few hours, she had retired early with her love back to the hotel room. Her brother, now thoroughly engaged in conversations, and alcohol consumption, had stayed with at the bar with his sisters friends.

After a night of what the sister had presumed to be friendly drinking, the older brother walked had returned to the hotel guest room, shirtless. He had, unfortunately, walked in on his sister and her boyfriend engaging in a bit of rough sexual relations. We discovered his sister's boyfriend happened to be a high school guidance counselor, and, when he had attempted to diffuse the situation prior to our arrival, the older brother had started to punch him. After pushing the boyfriend across the bed, the brother had proceeded to throw the counselor's luggage at him. Overall, it had not been a pleasant scenario that we had been called to, but

it was negotiable one, and we began to offer the distraught family several options of resolution.

A few moments into engaging and mediating the situation, we receive a call over our radios. The police had notified our dispatch that they tracked the man down from the bar he had come from, and were on the way up, to interrogate him, along with bar's chef. Hearing the call, the man reached down, swore some threats, and dumped the contents of his suitcase onto the other bed. As his behavior became more unpredictable, he, in Italian, he swore at his sister and told her to leave the room immediately.

She translated his words and chose to leave. As she did, on the way out, she held the door open for the police to enter the room. The police arriving and seeing the man looking through his belonging immediately withdrew their guns and ordered the man to the ground. Shocked, we in the security staff, rushed to remove ourselves from the line of fire, and pushed the boyfriend out of the room as we did.

Once the brother was subdued and handcuffed, a new, more frightening story emerged. The man, while in the bar had ordered a pizza for his new friends. He had given very specific instructions on how he wanted it to be cooked. When the pizza arrived, and it was not how he had ordered, he became irate. He demanded to speak to the chef. The chef, a bother-in-law of the owner, was less than courteous when he had received the

complaints. The chef used harsh language and expletives towards the man and told him to leave the bar.

The brother, now thoroughly inebriated, spat at the chef and was then gently escorted out by the bar's friendly bouncers. Angry, he stated that he had a gun in his hotel room and that he was going to come back to shoot the chef and his staff. It was later discovered that the man did have a gun in his possession; however, when the family checked in, he had left the baggage containing the fire arm was left in his sister's vehicle.

As he was placed under arrest, he made additional threats. Claiming love of his sister as a motive, he stated he wanted to kill her boyfriend, kill the chef's immediate family for the disrespect he had shown for himself and his family, kill the bar's owner, shoot the police, and kill all the staff at the bar. He claimed he was old school and would not be disrespected by anyone. Much to the genuine shame of the sister, he was carted off to the police cruiser.

CHAPTER 4

The Party Ain't Over Until…

The Heroin Addict

One of the main unfortunate aspects of any law enforcement position is that in reality, the occupation will call upon you to interact with and assist member of your society at their least honorable moments. Some of the most emotionally demanding situations occur when dealing with those who are genuinely attempting to be decent, however, are finding themselves to be in unfortunate situations. Despite the repetition of reprobate behavior, there are times when you lose the emotional distance which you mentally prepare yourself daily with, and interactions become genuinely personal.

One late, stormy Tuesday afternoon, I was dispatched to a guest room for a medical situation. A vendor attending a trade show convention had left the booth in the care of his mid-thirties son as he went to the room. He stated he was feeling dizzy and nauseous. When the man failed to return to his booth after an hour, his son called us to perform a welfare check on his father. His father answered the initial telephone call made to the guest room and said he felt absolutely terrible and wanted medical assistance. I was told he was experiencing stomach pains as well as flu like symptoms.

When I arrived at the room, in tow with all our available first aid equipment, the father, a man in his late fifties and with a weathered face, answered the door. He could barely stand and was doubling over in pain. I

wrapped my shoulder around his chest and lower shoulder and assisted him back to the bed. Stacking pillows behind his back for support, I assisted him in sitting in an upright position, then began to evaluate his medical condition.

He was not in good shape. He was sweating profusely, nauseous, was suffering from a migraine and a stuffy nose. His pillow sheet and comforters were sweat doused and I saw spots of blood on his moustache. He politely informed me that he was Hepatitis C positive, and I should wear the large black plastic medical gloves, attached to our bag. He repeated he was experiencing the Flu like symptoms which he had mentioned over the phone.

As I spoke to him, trying to determine the cause of his symptoms and the ailment afflicting him, he rolled onto the bed and curled into a fertile position, his back facing me. He seemed to be unable to look me directly in the face. I could see he was more emotionally disturbed than in physical pain.

He reluctantly and remorsefully expressed to me that his life was a constant repetition of backward spirals and despite his best efforts, he was destined for failure. He had overcome a heroin addiction, only to relapse, had gotten a steady job, only to underperform to be fired. He had created a business without establishing a local market for his products and now had to continuously travel to different trade shows to pedal his wares. He expressed that he felt as though he was losing his

permanent aspiration and motivation, the love and adoration of his son.

He had gone back to the room, with the objective of intentionally overdosing on the heroin he had brought with him, and committing suicide. In the end, he said, his only relief from a life of failure would be a quick death. He felt joyful that, though he could not control his life, he could determine his death. Though it brought him joy that it was his son who made the call to monitor his health, he continued in his misery.

He had already taken a small portion of heroin preceding my arrival. He had been experiencing the congestion and flu like symptom prior to his dosage, however, his other symptom appeared to be the result of a bad heroin ingestion. I was unable to communicate my hypothesis of ailment as the effects of the heroin began to control his mental capabilities. He remained on the bed crying, explaining his sorrows, and convulsing in bursts of confusion and pain.

Becoming emotionally attached when attempting to assist a troubled individual can distort clarity and prove useless in establishing a resolution, but the more the man rambled on, the more I began to realize he did not need financial, mental, or physical assistance, but an emotional connection to regain his connection to humanity.

I sat on a chair facing him and listened as he talked until I could convince him to get the medical and psychiatric help he desperately needed. When he finally

gave his permission, nearly forty five minutes into our interaction, the call for an ambulance was made.

When the first responders arrived, he responded to their questions with one words answers and grunts. As he was wheeled out, however, he looked back at me with the faintest of smiles. A thank you was briefly mouthed then his eyes went slowly to the ceiling above him. The passing moment of clarity and gratitude was interrupted by the drugs in his system.

A tragedy of the soul who's causation was the best of intentions. I believe, in many ways, he had allowed his own personal desires to effect his mental performances. This had led him to the doorway to death. What this man had craved for his entire life was success. Reckless ambition does not lead to personal success. The diligent organization of structured steps can be a pathway to gain.

Smokers

Being immersed in the law enforcement industry, by its own nature, allows a participant to experience many exhilarating and passionately charged scenarios. Situations and entire work days can, and often times, do change suddenly and without warning. This leads too many emotional experiences both during and after events occur.

One of the absolute worst emotional shifts I have received in my experiences in dealing with negative situations is watching as people undergo the penalties deserving of others. There is a price to pay for wrong doings. Unfortunately, time occur where the people surrounding the wrongdoer unjustly suffer. When these encounters do occur, there are never any personal feelings of self-fulfillment, gratification or elation for those enforcing the policies. This feeling of being forced to watch and participating in undeserving individual suffering is best exemplified through the next incident.

The convention itself was an enormous entertainment rally. Billboards and internet ads were set in place several months prior to the actual start date, and several entertainment celebrities, both local and national, were scheduled to both make appearances, to deliver speeches, provide question and answer sessions, and to provide photo shoot opportunities for celebrity fans.

Over twenty thousand had purchased tickets for a three day event. Not only was the hotel completely sold out, but also three of the additional surrounding hotels were booked to capacity. In addition, the local demographic was expected to bring in foot traffic which would purchase day tickets. These tickets were on schedule to bring in at least six thousand more curious thrill seekers throughout the event's three days. Portions of the road leading into the event were blocked off and additional hotel and parking became hellish.

Hundreds of vendors set up stands both inside and outside of the hotel. Although all of the vendors catered to their target market; each merchant boasted of something unique and exclusive to their shop. The competing market atmosphere created a perfect organized chaos as thousands of customers pushed themselves to receive their limited merchandise before it was sold out.

At the height of the event, a fire alarm sounds. The sound that came from the ceiling's loudspeakers surpassed the sound of the crowd's movements, chatters and cheers. Those of us assisting in crowd control, quickly radioed in to discover the cause of the alarm. We were informed our control panels indicated that there was a fire in the main electrical room and adjunct boiler room. These rooms require both a special hallway and staircase to access the basement of the hotel. If there was a fire, the lives of most of the attendees were in danger.

An emergency dispatch was issued for all available security officers and all engineering staff to immediately respond to the location of the situation. Emergency services were immediately notified. Within two minutes, seven security staff members and four engineers stampeded their way through the concerned bystanders to arrive at the scene.

When we arrived, we were fear stricken by the terrifying sight of smoke whisking from underneath the room's large metal doors. The decision was made to immediately evacuate all of the hotel floors as well as all participants at the convention for their own safety.

With a coordinated effort by the event security staff, the event administration staff, our hotel convention staff and engineering staff and our security staff, the convention and an estimated seven thousand people were displaced in less than approximately nine minutes from the observation of the smoke. All non-emergency hotel and event staff were escorted away to a safe distance.

Almost immediately as we dispersed the crowd, we were forced to clear a pathway surrounding the hotel's entrance for emergency fire vehicles and the police squad cruisers. We welcomed them, and hurriedly explained the situation as we guided them through the back hallways, to the location of the incident.

Fully believing the possibility of a full on electrical and boiler room fire, the firemen proceeded to dress in and respond in their full fire resistant uniform and gear.

Following our security staff members, they dragged the hoses from the nearest fire hose station, down the stairwell through the brick and mortar corridor to the very smoking door itself.

Myself, two other security guards, five engineers, and four police officers, followed some distance behind the fire responders to assist them in any way we could. Making note of the smoke, they thrust the door open, pushing in the hoses and made their entry.

We watched them produce an absolute twist of emotional disposition. Their faces turned from emblazoned passion and determination to shock and confusion. One put down his water hose, pulled off his face mask, and called us over to the doors. As his firefighting brothers followed in his unperturbed example, the police and ourselves, confused, made way over We found ourselves walking right into a raging stoner session of epic proportion.

Inside the room were eleven individuals, the oldest of which was thirty eight and youngest being sixteen, who after scouring the hotel for a good place to smoke their marijuana, found the empty basement and began smoking next to all the machines surrounding them.

Their smoking set off all the alarms inside of the rooms. Lights had flashed and alarms had sounded, but most were too stoned too care. They were lazing around watching the lights going off, until we terrified them with our entry. One younger Caucasian man, shirt off, initially

lying face down on the concrete floor, decided he would evade us by trying to blend in with the machines.

Not wanting to use his energy to stand, he belly rolled behind them, and began emitting his own beeping sounds. His comical response was what we needed to relieve the stress we had assumed due to our prior conviction of danger and many first responders and guards alike found themselves snickering at his reaction.

By the time we were able to discover and address the situation, escort the smokers to the police vehicles, contact the parents of the minors, reset our fire alarm systems, replace all fire resilient equipment back to the fire trucks, shut off the water flow established for the hoses, and coordinate with the event managers for attendees to proceed orderly back into the building, more than two and a half hours had passed.

Vendors and attendees were forced to forgo nearly three hours of the ten hours for which they paid for that day. Understandably irate, most demanded refunds for their lost time. Not only were we forced to console their emotional distress, but also thousands of lost dollars for both vendor sales and convention refunds. Tens of thousands of dollars were lost in both vendor sales and convention reimbursement due to the actions of the eleven smokers.

The Bad Tipper

There is a terrible truth to greed, while the Invisible Hand theory provided to mankind by a progressive Adam Smith in *The Wealth of Nations* (II) has provided humanity with a revolutionary catalyst for continual progression, selfishness, in and off itself, does not purely generate the success of an individual. The minimization expenses does lead to wealth retention, however, there is a fine line, when consuming, between managing money wisely and creating a financial jeopardy to crafts professionals. One's focus of self-progression should not hinder the successes of others working towards the same goals.

Like most fine cuisines, our luxury restaurant came fully equipped with exquisite and exotic wines and delicacies from around the nation and world. Our servers were trained in all the different specifics of the cuisines, including their preparation and origin. Most were just graduating culinary school or working towards their degrees in preparation for a career in the fine dining industry. They came to work every day prepared to both provide excellent customer service and to communicate their knowledge of their trade.

As is customary of businessmen, a younger foreign app creator invited an experienced American business developer out to a business dinner. Although they communicated several times email, this would be the first

time the two met in person. The purpose of the meeting was to discuss a possible partnership.

What the young creator did not know, prior to the dinner, was how thoroughly the business man had researched the young entrepreneurs' app designs. He had investigated and reviewed the designer's portfolio and his product enough to excite the businessman for the opportunity to offer a partnership opportunity. The business man came prepared to make an offer with a contract in his briefcase.

Hoping to win over the business developer's support via bribery, the creator ordered a rather expensive dinner arrangement and even more expensive champagne. The two toasted to each other's prior successes. Over time, the dinner conversation turned casual. As the two attempted to discover the other's temperament, the business developer, a member of the local community, greeted their waitress somewhat passionately and made several inquiries in regards to the menu.

As the dinner was coming to a close the bill which was around three thousand dollars was delivered to the young man for payment. The businessman took this as his cue and pulled out the contract and a novelty pen. He then went about explaining the rather lengthy agreement and the specifics of how he would assist the creator and what his business expectations were of the engineer.

Not wanting to interrupt their conversation, the waitress slipped the enclosed bill onto the table, and left

for the kitchen. The foreign technologist looked up swiftly, and, without a polite word to the waitress, stopped her, gave her his credit card for the bill and hurried her off. Back to business, the business developer resumed with his demands. Within moments, the check was returned, merger was fully explained, questions were answered, and the final strokes of the agreement were set to be completed.

The young man received the receipt, signed, put the bill cover back on the table and indicated he was ready to give it back to the waitress. Slightly taken aback, the businessman quipped "no tip today?" The young man did not comprehend that he was stepping into a baited trap. The waitress, I was later informed, was a member of the businessman's church. Her father was the church organist, and he was in fact, a quite popular individual in the congregation. The young man had not picked up on the subtle cues of familiarity between the two throughout the night. "Here the tip, work smart not hard", was the sneered reply.

The businessman politely disagreed, arguing that the lady had done a fine job. Despite their different opinions, and still looking for a compromise, the businessman politely offered to pay the tip since the young man payed for the expensive dinner. Loudly, the engineer said, "Fuck the tip, and fuck her, why are making an issue out of it?"

The businessman's smile dissipated. He calmly but swiftly removed the contract from the table and stood to

leave. He turned and looking the young man directly in the eye, he firmly remarked, "You're not the type of man that men like me do business with", and walked off with his offer and opportunity.

A few minutes later we get the call, the young man is silently crying and continues to sit at the abandoned table. He was disturbing the other patrons by refusing to leave. We were called to physically remove him. He initially attacked us verbally to save his shattered dignity and we understood his devastation no matter how well deserved.

The manner you present yourself through your actions will be the manner you are perceived to be. The man had excellent craftsmanship. Nonetheless, the blatant inconsiderateness of his demeanors had left him without a business partner or financial backing. He was left humiliated in front of an audience.

Best Intentions, Worst Behavior

Guests do not check their medical problems at the door. Although most of the medical calls we were asked to respond to, happened to be the culmination, or active development of many combined symptom, immediate emergencies can do happen without notice and occur on a frequent basis in the hotel industry. They bring out natural instincts of personal care and protection from both the responder and the sufferer.

As a responder, you often feel an innate sense of urgency that must be channeled properly to provide the best care. Although there were several instances when the medical procedural response could have been improved, the next incident stood out to me from the immediate momentary public embarrassment then, later, the hilarity that resulted from the situation.

The assemblage was a small private art exhibition and auction. I am have just finished relieving a coworker, who is working behind the stage, for his lunch break. His assignment was to provide asset protection for the prized pieces about to be displayed. We were standing together and conversing about the grandeur of the items; most of which were uncovered and set to be brought to the stage.

In front of us, a wide wooden stage and podium has been erected. It's minimalized by an enormous velvet curtain, shrouding the items yet to be displayed and

keeping the expecting crowd in anticipation. A massive projector displays the items from all angles as they are presented.

A career auctioneer is out front, with his normal exhibition crew, rapidly hyping potential customers into the sale. Only one person, an expert in fine art transportation and a member of the auctioneer's company is allowed backstage to retrieve the art pieces for display.

I suddenly hear the auctioneer stop his steady rambling and gasp into the microphone. As I make my way towards the stage to investigate, one of the hotel's event managers runs behind the curtain, on his way to an emergency hotel phone. When I approached him to discover his intentions, he tells me to rush to the podium and informed me one of the auctioneer's staff members has collapsed on stage. I hastily follow the event manager up and radio for another agent to assist me by bringing the medical bag to the location.

As we cross the curtain and run the ramp to the stage, I see the fallen man on the side of the stage. He is mid-fifties and is lying on his side, semiconscious, heavily spewing bile. Vomit is coursing through his long silver hair, the crowd murmurs in a disturbed hush, and the frightened auctioneer is pacing in nervous circles behind him. The event's developer attempts to force an intermission and show the crowd into the hall but most stayed to watch the action.

Seeking to avoid a choking hazard, I quickly lift the man to sit upright. Though he is sweating profusely, he is involuntarily shivering. His lips quiver as he grabs my arm, and attempts to speak to me. Vomit coats my knee as I kneel to keep him vertical, and listen to his speech. The auctioneer, whom I later find out is also the man's romantic partner, quietly relays to another of his staff member, who in turn, informs me that the man is diabetic, and hadn't eaten for the last six hours. From all of his apparent symptoms, it appeared as though the man was going into diabetic shock.

The medical bag is brought by brought by an elderly female coworker. She is a retired career paramedic, who had been on the first responder force for nearly thirty years. Though extremely diligent and thorough in her profession, she is notoriously sharp tongued and goal focused, but in a moment where time was of the essence I was initially relieved to see it was her who responded.

As I begin to inform her of the situation, I update her of the auctioneer's relation to the man. She interrupts the anxious auctioneers walk, in order to question to him. We needed to discover the sufferer's current medications, prior medical history, and all other related information we need to properly assist the auctioneer's partner.

She turns his attention away from the man so that he can focus on answering the questions, and they walk

together towards the center of the stage. Just as the auctioneer begins to explain the man's prior medical history directly to my coworker, she stops him in midsentence. "FUCCKKK, YOU LEFT YOUR FUCKKIN' MIC ON" she yells at the sound operator. The surround sound system blares her expletive throughout the convention hall and into the hallway.

Attempting to save face, I turn quickly to tell her to watch her language, but I can already hear gasps and chuckles of the attendees. I motion for her to come to me and send her back to the banquet's office to retrieve a fruit juice bottle for the man. Though barely conscious, and having trouble speaking, my patient finds humor in the situation, and, coughs a couple of chuckles at my obvious embarrassment.

She returns a few minutes later sprinting back with a bottle of fruit juice, a premade tortilla wrap, and a candy bar. Together with his lover, we cut the food into small portions and coach the collapsed man into eating the food.

Once the sugar settles, he stabilizes. His strength begins to return and he is able to stand on his power. EMS arrives and begins to check his vitals. He is cleared by the medical professionals. Heart felt claps of joy and relief echo across the stage from the audience as we assist the man gingerly walk off stage. He declines any further medical attention, and we escort him to his room for self-assisted medication.

The next day, I'm called into the director of operations office. The hotel's coordinator of the event is there, as well my security director, the client, and the director of banquets. The coworker is brought in a few minutes later, by another security manager and an awkward retelling story of the event beginning from its genesis and ending at its conclusion commences to unfold.

I find out that my coworker, while dealing with the situation, ran to the back and grabbed the first food items she came across from off of the banquets counter. She then proceeded to curse out the banquet staff who attempted to block her exit. The banquets manager became extremely irritated at both her unprofessional response and the fact that the items she had grabbed had been prepared for another guest of the hotel. The manager had to call the guest, inform her of a delay in the kitchen as the cook hurried to remake the food they had just prepared.

The banquets director after being informed of her intentions, and the situation which had occurred in the convention hall, was only disturbed that she hadn't approached the banquet manager and communicated her intentions at the time of the occurrence. The items would have been provided immediately and the pointless verbal altercation could have been completely avoided. The client also complained of her use of profanity on stage, but she also humorously remarked, most of the audience had complimented her for an exciting show.

Some of the customers had remarked that it had been the most exciting art exhibit they had attended and that they would be returning customers.

Despite her good intentions of caring for the injured man, she was fired for inappropriate behavior. Irate at being fired after participating in saving a man's life, she cursed out the directors, myself, and even the client. While being escorted off the premises, she proceeded to spit on as much of the property as she and successfully destroyed all prior business relationships

Four days later, I am called into the office. Once the auctioneer arrived home, he went online to praise the swift actions and personalized care his partner received. Additionally, he had sent a three hundred dollars as a tip. As the management staff, no longer wanted to interact with my former coworker, I was given the full amount.

Premature Celebration

On occasion, a good member of staff, on advancement to leader, may lose direction and hinder or damage the performance of the employees they are leading.

Occupational advancement and attainment of leadership based purely on prior job performances at an entry level position, does not necessarily dictate exceptional managerial behavior or blameless leadership.

There was an elderly bartender who worked in the hotel's upscale hostelry for nearly eight years. He was well liked among management, his fellow staff members, and guests alike. He was semi-retired and had worked in several different industries prior to bartending. His relaxed and uniquely varied choice of clothes displayed his casual demeanor and his specialty was guest service and communication.

When people visited the bar as a guest, he would pay attention to them as if they were a friend. His personality earned him a very decent living, and he often ended his shift with several hundred dollars in tips which he would generously distribute among the bar backs and fellow staff. As a fellow employee, he was always there to hear them out and to provide experienced counsel.

After being offered and declining management roles on several occasions, the position of bar manager

opened. The position would allow for nearly complete control of the bar during its hours of operations. When the regions general manager, himself, came to our elderly bartender, and asked that he consider applying for the position, he decided he would lead his fellow bar staff.

After the official offer and acceptance became public knowledge, he convened a pre-shift meeting to deliver his promotional speech. He had told his staff that he was close to completely retiring and he felt as though he could groom a worthy manager to precede him by personal demonstration of character. Needless to say, the bar staff was ecstatic to have him as a leader and many already saw him as a mentor.

Three days after he delivered the official announcement of his promotion, he decided to throw a celebratory after hour's private party for the bar staff. When they arrived to work that afternoon, he informed all of his former staff mates, including the DJ, a contractor with his own personal equipment to wait until after the bar was closed, then bring a plus one to have the final party of the night. It was announced to be both a celebration of his promotion and gesture of appreciation for staff's hard work.

I happen to be working in the dispatch office that night. As was the normal procedure, at the set time, I received the call from the new manager, that the bar was ready to be closed. Agents were dispatched, the last few partiers were walked out for the night, the bar was shut down. The liquor is taken to the proper location, and I

log the necessary closing information into the computer system. Assuming the staff would be cleaning the tables and closing the bar's tabs before they left, I removed my focus from watching the cameras in the bar, and began watching the cameras on the floors for unusual activity.

About an hour and half later, after dealing with a few instances of drunk and disorderly guests, non-sanctioned guest room parties, and steadily watching the CCTV cameras in the hotel, I see movement in the bar, and glance over to their monitors just in time to witness several individuals, walking into the bar. I see the bartenders resume service, and start pouring the new patrons drinks. Extremely unfamiliar, I send staff members to investigate the situation.

They find the newly promoted manager, sitting in front of his wife on one of the bar stools. He had lost control of his celebration, and of his sobriety and he was leaning forward onto the counter. A few drinks lay directly in front of him on both the floor and the countertop. As the bar manager was too inebriated to communicate legibly, the security manager, as the operations of bar was under the general oversight of the hotel, decided to request the presence of the hotel's general night manager for direction.

Several of the bar staff had created an electrifying party. Despite the fact liquor that bottles had been placed on the turntables, in the background, dance music pushed the party goers into utopian psychological states. The bar's liquor room was left opened so as to allow the

party goers to choose their own liquors, and there were several non-employees enjoying an extraordinary carnival.

Knowing many of the security guards by name, the former bartender attempted to include them in the merrymaking atmosphere. He called them over and requested his staff to bring drinks be brought out for the guards. Four of the non-employees, believing that the situation was acceptable, went into the liquor and drunkenly wheeled a Queen Mary Cart filled with different goodies, for the hotel manager, security manager and guards to make their selections.

When the managers and guards politely refused to partake, referencing the fact they were at work, and asked the liquor to be returned to the storage room's shelves, several of the invited non-employees began to take offense at their behavior. They started using profanities towards the security staff. A young woman, got in the hotel manager's face and informed him she would slap him if he attempted to shut the party down, another man, tried to flip the Queen Mary Cart and the bottles on it over, but fell, drunk and laughing, to the ground, as it proved too much too heavy for him.

Sensing the tensions rising, the wife of the newly manager, a former professor of law, started to attempt to make her way with her husband towards the door. When she was unable to convince him to stand to leave, she attempted to regain control of their party. After knocking on a glass with a spoon, calmly informed the

party attendees that the party was over, and asked them to leave.

Most of the party-goers, were unaware of who she was and the initial reason behind the festivities, so they booed her. Temper's flared, and after another threat of violence, the hotel manager demanded that all participants unwilling to leave of their own accord to be physically removed. Several of the bar staff members, now thoroughly ashamed at the way their friends behaved at their place of employment, hoping to retain their jobs, demanded that their friends leave.

After more than eight years of service inside of the bar as an employee, the new manager was let go, not a week after his promotion. His desire to mold a great leader to follow in his footsteps was cut short, and many of his would be followers were released for their participation and the behaviors of their friends.

Appropriate management does include strength of integrity, even if it means unpopularity. The former bartender had made several erroneous blunders in judgement that night and had allowed his desires for popularity and merriment overshadow his sense of responsibility. The error proved costly for himself and the people he had worked for nearly a decade.

CHAPTER 5

Kumbaya

Prelude

When You Think No One Is Watching has, thus far, provided you the reader with a small taste of the complex and sometimes irrational mixing bowl which luxury hotel and resort workers face on a daily basis within the bounds of their employment. These wild but true stories have been based, up to this point, on both the absurdity and wickedness of the individuals I have observed and intermingled with

However, I want to assure you that these stories, for the most part, have stuck a permanent place in my mind because of their rarity of occurrences. One fact that I have gained from the observation and conversations I have held with a broad range of individuals originating from all sorts of differing demographics, is that most rational people truly desire to be admired and adored for their good conduct and personal success. People, for the most part, give their absolute greatest efforts when attempting to better themselves. This, in turn, usually betters the lives of those that they chose to surround themselves with.

There have also been those who have gone out of their own way, some have even placed themselves in danger or have accepted losses, in order to care for others. These are their stories:

The Doctor And The Cook

To show its appreciation for its staff, a local hospitable threw a gala for its employees. Doctors, nurses, physicians and their assistants, as well as various other hospitable staff members, were pampered with a comedy show, a raffle with various gift cards and hospitable memorabilia, and a custom dinner. At each table, a personal chef was situated, with a culinary station to prepare a dinner of the guests choosing. The planned ending, immediately following the dinner, was a 1980's throwback disco dance hall set up at another ballroom. The invitees were admonished to wear eighties styled dress attire.

One younger doctor came accompanied by his wife, a nurse practitioner at a private firm. After placing their orders from the provided menu, they sat back to watch the cook prepare their dishes. Unfamiliar with many of his new coworker, the doctor and his wife had sat at a long table with one other couple, hoping others would voluntarily come and join them for the pleasantries of the evening. The chef, quickly realizing their seclusion, began a conversation with the couple as he set about a skillful and entertaining gourmet performance.

Becoming distracted by the specifics of the conversation, the chef cut deep into his own hand. The cook turned away from his hot stove, held his hand to

his chest. He quickly balled his hand into a fist, gasping from the pain as he did. The immediacy of the incision jolted the emotions of the cook. He looked down frozen in place, holding his hand in shock, as his blood seeped onto the dish he was preparing.

The doctor quickly dawned his suit jacket and dress shirt. As other chef's and banquet employees radioed the location of the emergency, requesting that we bring medical equipment, the doctor laid the stunned man on his back. Elevating his hand, the young physician had his wife wrap the chef's hand using the doctor's personal undershirt. The young doctor continued in his prior conversation with the cook, hoping to relieve his panic. He asked specified questions in regards to their conversation to keep the chef's mind off of the pain.

The doctor stood shirtless in the middle of the gala surrounded by his new coworkers and peers until we arrived to properly wrap the chef's hand. But even then, he provided his professional input and asked procedural medical questions, as we wrapped the cook's hand. He gave no regard to the festivities he had come to enjoy. When the paramedics arrived, he followed us to the ambulance, providing the suitable medical information he had just acquired, to them.

His kindness did not go unnoticed, when he returned to the festivities, the company had ordered a bottle of champagne for the man and his wife, but the couple politely refused the gesture. The doctor had done

the good deed for the sake of doing well, and he did not want recognition for his actions.

Motherly Love

There is something miraculous about the love of a mother. Women who have had children often demonstrate a pure well-meant desire to see others be better, despite what detriment may come their way as a result of their kindness. This purity of love can alter the worst of sceneries and soften the most complex of dilemmas.

The resort was a frequent destination for many special needs camps. It offered both a comfortable and contained environment, where adaptable commodities were easily accessible. In addition, it held a large pool and adjoining recreational facility with an arcade which often proved to be a favorite destination for many of the children.

The surrounding suburbs offered many tourist attractions, exhibits, and museums that were often incorporated in the arranged schedule as day trips. When the children would return from the exhibitions, they would find many of the meeting rooms had been adapted for other various delights and activities. Parents who chose to send their children through the programs often chose to be returning customers.

On one winter retreat for the handicap, a blizzard struck the region. Most of the children were able sleep, however, a few, some afraid, and some inspired, stayed

up to watch the piling heaps of snow fall throughout the night.

All but snowed in, a few residents of the local community chose to shovel their way over and stay in our dually back up generated facility. In addition to our luxurious interior, we offered many conveniences, such as heat, clean water, fresh food, and internet that would be inaccessible elsewhere throughout the storm.

Two of guests were a young couple, mid-twenties, with a seven month's year old baby. The baby was not yet fully sleeping nights and, as the baby tossed in the night, the mother, not getting any sleep, chose to walk with her toddler around the hotel. Rocking her baby in her arms, the mother began soothing her cry's as she walked the hotels differing entertaining levels.

She encountered us in the lobby. A severely autistic female teen, who was barely able to speak, was standing by the entrance's glass doors shrieking in panic as the snowed piled higher. Three camp counselors, worn out from their travels throughout the day prior to the snow, were doing their best to console her. One of the teen's male counselors, semi awake, was emulating relaxation by example. He was sitting behind her in a fold up chair, struggling against exhaustion, attempting to calm her down by reasoning with her. We were standing behind the counselors attempting to assist them any way needed.

A young mother calmly walked between us and the autistic child. Her young baby confused now, had

stopped its crying to watch what was going on. After asking for permission to assist, the mother leaned in and said nothing but comforting words to the young lady, rubbing her back as she spoke.

Whether she established a more convincing demonstration of affection, or whether the suffering teen felt safer in the presence of a mother, I will never know, but the child listened to the mother's words. The young lady, somewhat comforted, stopped shrieking, and pressed her face against the cold glass window pane. Tears filled her eyes as she watched the ground disappear to winter's grasp.

The mother motioned for us to bring a chair so she could sit next to her. The exhausted counselor got out of his own chair, picked it up, and walked it over to the mother. Standing behind her, the young camp counselor watched her relax the troubled teen.

Later, the teenager removed herself from the window and lay down on the cold marble floor. Slowly, she crawled behind the mother's fold up chair for personal protection, staring at the mother's daughter as she did.

The young mother sat with the girl for nearly two hours. Giving up the room and the rest that she had paid for, she sat till the young lady fell asleep and could be placed in a wheelchair and carried to her room.

She provided an example of compassion for the trained camp leaders to follow. Neither the hotel staff

nor the camping staff knew the young lady, prior to the experience. She didn't receive any offers of gain for her sacrifice. She appeared satisfied to offer the extension of motherly love the girl needed.

Lover Conquers Hate

In the United States today, there is unfortunately a great racial divide that is routinely reopened due to the disrespect of origins, cultures, and values of other American citizens. Despite the numerous propositions and movements, there still exist and intolerance for differences.

An established group of indigenous Native Americans living throughout the United States announced an open event where members of the local community and hotel guests could join in ancient ceremonies and a cultural appreciation meetings. They offered a dinner that would include Native culinary dishes. The communal styled dinner would be followed by speeches from Native community leaders and organizers.

Showing utter disrespect, a mid-twenties Caucasian male came to the event sporting a Mohawk, a Redskin's jersey with the words, "Injun Pimp'", stitched in large lettering into the fabric. He had the disrespectful shirt tucked into a large brown belt which held up his torn jeans. Interestingly, the man decided on Jordan's as his choice in footwear.

The young man proceeded to move his way from the back entrance and sit in the front row directly behind the Native community leaders and event organizers. Initially, he did not verbally interact with or disturb the

other attendees, but his disrespectful choice of attire grabbed the attention of several guests at the event. Murmurs of disproval rose around him and into the ears of the event organizers.

Naturally, taking offense when they were informed of the young man actions, the group's organizers asked the mortified hotel event planning staff to resolve the situation. We were called by the hotel event manager to assist in removing the young man from the conference.

Much to our surprise, when we arrived to the ballroom, fully prepared to escort the man out, a group of Native leaders met us at the meeting room door to stop us. They informed us that they wanted him to stay and to learn their culture. However they too displayed indignation at his choice of attire. They stated that they wanted the man to remove his shirt by himself.

As we went to the young man to inform him of the organizer's preference, we observed that we had received an audience of onlookers. Knowing the situation may be confrontational, two of the security guards stood by the chair aisle. I and another guard moved through the crowd to speak with the man.

When informed of the wishes of the event organizers and asked for his cooperation, the man outright refused to remove his shirt. He said he was from out of state; however, and as a guest of the hotel his sole purpose was to intentionally disturb and disrupt the event. He proceeded to spout out white supremacist rhetoric.

Sitting directly in front of the man, an older Native leader, unmoved by the white supremacist's hateful remarks, turned to the man with a smile and said, "There is no need for selfishness here, this meeting was meant for the two of us" the older man stated.

The young man violently responded to older man's cool demeanor. He balled his fist and swung at the elderly man, hitting his neck and ear. Enraged, another Caucasian male in his thirties and attending the conference with his Hispanic wife, jumped toward the young man and shoulder shoved him towards the door. The second man began grabbing at his shirt attempting to wrestle him down. As I and other guards jumped into separate the pair, the offensive jersey was almost completely torn off the first man.

Now bruised and fully enraged, the white supremacist began a verbal rampage of curses and hate filled rhetoric towards the staff, the man attacking him, the locals attending the event and the Native American community.

The diplomatic meeting was now almost completely disrupted. Several of the men stood to their feet, prepared to fight as the young man began to shout about the superiority of his own race, and the savagery of the Native American people and incompetency of the staff. The second man's wife followed him into the hallway and cheers erupted for the couple.

As we pushed the young man out of the meeting room, we were followed by the elderly Native leader the

man had punched. After the removal process was complete, and we stood at the hotel's front drive, the young man now began to seek compensation from the hotel and the convention for the shirt which had been ripped off of him. The elderly man offered to give him his personal shirt, but the young man refused. He made the claim that he didn't want a spirit cursed shirt to be on his pure skin.

The police had been called by several attendees. When they arrived, the young man continued with his hate filled rhetoric towards one of the African American officers. When he was informed he was no longer welcome at the facility, he refused to vacate stating he had been a victim of assault. The second man denied his assertion.

Notwithstanding the hatred which had been directed towards him and his community, the Native leader never once responded in kind. He gave every opportunity to help the young man and to expand his knowledge and to purge his negative biases.

The convention resumed itself, despite the man's attempt of interruption and many found encouragement from the direction of event's organizers. They did not bash the man in the proceeding speeches, but instead used him as an example to thank those who came to support them. Although the young man had refused their advice, a showing of understanding and wisdom prevailed over self-imposed superiority and hatred.